STRATEGY FOR THE 60's

STRATEGY
FOR THE 60's

Edited by **JAY H. CERF** *and* **WALTER POZEN**

With an Introduction by **SENATOR J. W. FULBRIGHT**

Prepared by the

Foreign Policy Clearing House

FREDERICK A. PRAEGER, *Publisher*
New York

BOOKS THAT MATTER

Published in the United States of America in 1961
by Frederick A. Praeger, Inc., Publisher
64 University Place, New York 3, N.Y.

Copyright © 1960 by the Foreign Policy Clearing House, Inc.

Library of Congress Catalog Card Number: 61-12699

STRATEGY FOR THE 60's is published in two editions:

    A Praeger Paperback (PPS-51)

    A clothbound edition

Manufactured in the United States of America

CONTENTS

FOREWORD

No more systematic or far-reaching foreign policy research effort has ever been undertaken by Congress than the series of studies commissioned in 1959 by the Committee on Foreign Relations of the United States Senate. By the summer of 1960, this effort had resulted in thirteen major reports prepared by leading foreign policy research centers of the United States. The final products total 1431 fine-print pages.

In the present document, the Foreign Policy Clearing House has synthesized and summarized the findings and recommendations of the thirteen Senate studies. Our purpose has been to increase the accessibility of these comprehensive reports, not only to the U.S. policy makers for whom they were primarily intended, but also to those segments of the American public concerned with the critical foreign and defense policy areas which were under study.

This project will be successful if it achieves the following aims: (a) if it leads to a wider knowledge of the broad goals, premises and conclusions found in the source documents, and (b) if it motivates readers to return to the primary sources for the knowledge-in-depth which only they provide. While we feel that these are by no means modest aims, it is important to emphasize that this document in no way presumes to be a substitute, in whole or in part, for the source documents.

It has been a special concern of the Clearing House to preserve the integrity of the original studies. In each case, we submitted our product to the authors of the studies. In each case, the authors approved. For this helpful participation we extend our sincere thanks to Dr. Carl Marcy and the staff of the Senate Committee on Foreign Relations, as well as to each of the twelve major foreign policy research centers which produced the basic documents.

The Clearing House is indebted to numerous other specialists and institutions across the country for their generous assistance in preparing this publication. A grant from the Institute for International Order and the special consideration of Earl D. Osborn and George A. Beebe of that foundation were largely responsible for preparation of the manuscript. It is unlikely, moreover, that publication could have occurred without the assistance of the Mary S. Voorhees Company and that of Frank Altschul, W. L. Clayton, and Ralph I. Straus.

We are grateful to Morton Halperin of the Harvard Center for International Affairs for preparing the basic draft of the synthesis and to Dr. Ernest W. Lefever for his substantial contribution to our final method of approach. We are also indebted to Andrew E. Rice and Carol M. Cerf for their expert help in editing and re-editing.

Finally, the Advisory Board and Executive Committee of the Foreign Policy Clearing House gratefully acknowledge the able help of the FPCH staff and research consultants. These include the Associate Director and Counsel, Walter Pozen, as well as Noëlle B. Beatty, Winifred Armstrong, Janet Dorsch, and Lois Sidenberg.

JAY H. CERF
Director, Foreign Policy Clearing House

GLOSSARY OF ABBREVIATIONS USED IN THE TEXT

Originating Group   *Abbreviation*

1. Corporation for Economic
   and Industrial Research, Inc..CEIR

2. Stanford Research Institute..SRI

3. Foreign Policy Research Institute,
   University of Pennsylvania..FPRI

4. Program of African Studies,
   Northwestern University ....Northwestern

5. Conlon Associates, Ltd..Conlon

6. Maxwell Graduate School of Citizenship
   and Public Affairs, Syracuse University...............................Maxwell

7. Council on Foreign Relations, Inc....................................Council on Foreign
                                                                             Relations

8. Washington Center of Foreign Policy Research,
   The Johns Hopkins University..Johns-Hopkins

9. The Brookings Institution..Brookings

10. Center for International Affairs,
    Harvard University ....Harvard Center

11. A Harvard-Columbia Research Group under
    the administration of Columbia University.........................Harvard-Columbia

12. Center for International Studies,
    Massachusetts Institute of Technology.................................MIT

13. Staff, Committee on Foreign Relations,
    U.S. Senate ....Senate Staff

INTRODUCTION

. Almost two years ago, the Senate Committee on Foreign Relations, of which I am privileged to be Chairman, contracted with some of America's leading foreign-policy research institutions for a series of comprehensive studies of U.S. foreign and defense policies, with particular emphasis on the challenges and needed U.S. responses in the 1960's. The Committee's project was undertaken in order to assist it in the discharge of its duties in the field of foreign policy.

The United States constitutional system, in marked contrast to parliamentary systems of government, divides certain foreign-policy responsibilities between the executive and the legislative branches of the government. Thus, the President can *ask* that Congress declare war, but only Congress can *declare* war; the President can request funds for the conduct of foreign policy, but only the Congress can appropriate funds; the President can nominate ambassadors and negotiate treaties, but ambassadors must be confirmed in office, and treaties can only become effective with the approval of the Senate.

The Committee on Foreign Relations is the principal instrumentality to which the Senate turns for advice in the discharge of its constitutional duties in the field of foreign policy. In order to operate effectively, the Committee needs ideas, background, and information originating from sources outside the government. Congressional committees concerned with legislation in fields of domestic policy have available to them the wealth of ideas and information generated by the domestic press, by domestic organizations, and by constituents generally. In the field of foreign policy, however, it is the executive branch of the government which has a near monopoly on information and ideas. This is attributable in part to the fact that the Department of State has some 20,000 employees in daily contact with countries and individuals throughout the world.

The Committee on Foreign Relations has a close working relationship with the Department of State, which has been most cooperative in helping the Committee with its tasks. It is too much to expect, however, that the Department should expend its energy in obtaining for, and supplying to, the Committee information and ideas which may not be consistent with departmental views. This is not to say that the Committee seeks information and ideas for the purpose of opposing positions taken by the Department. We do believe, however, that U.S. policies may be strengthened by the Committee if it is in a position to test these policies against views which may not always correspond to those held by the Department.

Although the Committee in its work makes extensive use of the daily and periodic press, seeks the views of American citizens who may have had experience abroad, and encourages its members to seek firsthand information by study missions abroad, it has found the material obtained by studies of the type summarized here of immense value to its deliberations.

Although these studies were completed some months ago, subsequent events have indicated their value and corroborated the validity of many of their conclusions.

I attach the greatest importance to these studies. They contain what is probably the most comprehensive current analysis of the foreign-policy challenges confronting United States policy-makers in the years ahead.

If there was a major defect in the original reports, it was caused by the fact that few of our problems are simple. As a consequence, the reports total 1,431 printed pages. I suspect that the number of members of Congress or the executive branch who will find time to read these pages in full is rather limited.

To meet this problem, a private organization, the Foreign Policy Clearing House, has undertaken on its own initiative and responsibility to prepare and publish summaries and an analysis of the thirteen Committee studies. I believe that members of the Congress and of the executive branch, the public, students of foreign policy, and perhaps even some of our friends overseas will find this publication helpful in understanding the many problems that beset the conduct of the foreign policy of the United States.

Two points should be stressed. First, summaries are no substitute for the full understanding that can best come from reading the studies themselves, all of which were prepared by competent and careful students in specialized fields. Second, while the studies were prepared for use by the Committee on Foreign Relations and to assist it in the preparation of a final report to the Senate, it must be understood that the Committee has always held itself free to accept or to reject the findings and recommendations of the organizations and institutions which prepared studies for the Committee.

The Foreign Policy Clearing House is to be commended for its initiative in preparing these summaries.

J. W. FULBRIGHT
Chairman, Committee on Foreign Relations, U.S. Senate

I. THE CHALLENGES AND THE OPPORTUNITIES OF THE 1960's

All thirteen studies on American foreign policy, prepared for the Senate Foreign Relations Committee, agree that the United States, acting within the limits set by the forces at work within the twentieth century, can exert a major influence on the events of the next decade. This opportunity highlights two major American needs. First, a willingness to deal with the problems of the era in active and resourceful ways. Second, a greater understanding by the executive, the legislature, and the public of the processes at work in the world and of the effective means available to channel these processes toward ends that we value.

The major challenges facing the United States stem from three basic world trends: the emergence of the underdeveloped nations, the continuing Sino-Soviet threat, and the rapid advances in technology.

The *first major challenge* relates to the role of the emerging nations, a role already well symbolized by their new importance in the United Nations General Assembly. The path chosen by these new states in the next few years will directly affect the future shape of world civilization. Should they remain outside the Soviet camp, United States security and the cause of human freedom will have been vastly enhanced. Should they take the road of totalitarianism and Communism, the world will be a much more dangerous place for the United States. Although the choice will be made largely by the developing countries themselves, American policy can have a crucial influence on the end result.

The *second major challenge* facing the United States is the Sino-Soviet threat. The studies all hold that Communist hostility to the free world will continue over the next decade and far beyond. While Communist tactics may shift, the Sino-Soviet menace will be a continuing one that the United States and its allies will have to meet at all levels—diplomatic, military, economic and ideological. The existence of the Soviet Union and China makes the future of the underdeveloped areas even more precarious than it would be in any case. Unless the underdeveloped countries can be convinced that democracy and rapid economic growth are not incompatible, they are likely to choose the readily available model of Communism.

1

The *third major challenge* facing the United States in the 60's is posed by the growing destructive power of thermonuclear weapons and intercontinental rockets and the increasing number of nations possessing these weapons. The United States must continue to develop adequate military forces to deter both large-scale and local Communist aggression, but it must also begin seriously and vigorously to pursue a policy of arms control which could reduce the dangers of warfare in the thermonuclear age.

Vast opportunities will accompany these challenges over the next decade. As this period begins, the United States still has considerable prestige in the underdeveloped areas of the world. It has an opportunity to use its prestige to help develop effective and democratic governments in Africa, Asia, and Latin America. If the United States seizes this opportunity, it can make a major contribution to the stability of the world and the advancement of American goals. If it fails, the likely outcome is Communist domination.

The threat of world destruction through thermonuclear weapons presents not only a challenge but an opportunity. Despite their extensive disagreements, it is clear that neither the United States nor the Soviet Union could profit from a major thermonuclear war. Upon this fact rests the opportunity for effective arms control and for the channeling of disputes into more peaceful arenas.

In order to meet these challenges and to use these opportunities, the studies agree that the U.S. must have its national goals and purposes clearly in mind. Our primary goal is to maintain a free and democratic society within the borders of the United States. In addition, we are interested in the spread of democracy and freedom to other areas of the world, both for their own sake and in the interests of American security.

The challenges and the opportunities of the 60's can be clearly and simply stated, but appropriate policies and machinery of policy formulation are far less easy to define. It is to these difficult tasks that the studies herein summarized address themselves.

II. THE CHALLENGE OF THE EMERGING NATIONS

A massive revolt against poverty is currently under way in Africa, Asia, the Middle East, and Latin America. For the first time, there is a widespread belief that something can be done to lessen the hunger, disease, and illiteracy which accompany poverty. The new leaders and their newly emerging nations are nonetheless caught in a great paradox. At the very moment that they want to eliminate outside ties with industrial countries, which are reminiscent of political subordination, they must turn to these countries for economic and technical help.

Because these countries need and ask for help, they suddenly occupy a pivotal position in the struggle between the Soviet Union and the United States. In competing for the loyalties of peoples of Asia and Africa, the Russians have certain immediate advantages. They pose as liberators from Western colonialism. They malign the United States for its ties with colonial powers. They point to the discrimination against Negroes in the United States. Meanwhile they offer their own technical achievements as proof that Communism is the way to rapid economic growth. Consequently the United States must develop a program which permits self-respect to the peoples of the emerging nations and leads to economic growth without resort to Communism.

An integrated, effective American program for the underdeveloped areas must be based on an understanding of the process of development and growth. Of the 13 Senate reports, the study by the Center for International Studies of the Massachusetts Institute of Technology presents the most extensive discussion of the problems of economic growth. MIT's view of the growth process is briefly reviewed here as background to other Senate reports which deal with the role of outside aid in economic development.

"The evolution of societies," the MIT study states, "occurs through the interaction of a myriad of factors, conveniently summed up under such labels as economics, politics, sociology, psychology . . . The transition to modernity has occurred simultaneously in many countries, each with its own particular history, resource endowment, class structure, political system, and so to attempt to generalize about the process of economic, social and political change in the underdeveloped countries might appear as a risky exercise.

"And yet, generalization is essential if we wish to understand and to cope with the problems which the revolution of modernization presents."

In almost all underdeveloped countries, several factors make rapid evolution difficult. The MIT study emphasizes that economic development cannot proceed without accompanying social, political and psychological development. Generally speaking, the major *economic* need is for capital investment to increase productive capacity. At some stages of development, we can also anticipate a critical requirement for foreign exchange to make possible purchases of capital equipment from more developed areas.

In the *social* field, there is a need for trained elites who are prepared to assume the vital administrative roles in the developing countries. Also needed are social institutions to replace the closed-family systems typical of underdeveloped countries. Unless these problems are solved, the social upheavals accompanying economic development are likely to act as a serious brake on progress.

With the need for changes in the economic and social fabrics of underdeveloped societies is a corresponding need to develop effective *political* institutions for modernization. There must be acceptance of the shift of political power from the village to the city and to elected leaders. Political interest groups and opposing political parties must emerge.

Cutting across the necessary changes in political, social and economic structures is the need to alter the *psychological* outlook of the people. The MIT study points out that even the leaders of underdeveloped societies seemingly committed wholeheartedly to development may experience psychological blocks to vigorously pushing the development process. The desire of the masses for economic growth and political maturity frequently conflicts with the psychological needs formerly fulfilled within the closed, ordered, traditional society from which they are emerging.

In considering American aid to developing countries, it is necessary to examine each country in the light of these four factors to determine what stage of development it has reached. The MIT study suggests four categories of countries, ranging from those just emerging from traditional patterns to those, such as India, Turkey and Argentina, that are close to becoming modern, industrial states. It stresses the importance of differentiating these states and providing different aid to them at different stages of development. It is only by considering carefully the needs of individual countries that the tools of American diplomacy can be effectively used in aiding the development process.

Economic Assistance Policy

All the studies make clear that the emerging nations will need substantial amounts of economic aid in order to become industrialized. Outside capital, however, is not likely to be effective except under certain conditions:

1) *The United States must encourage the emerging states to formulate long-range plans for balanced economic, political, and social growth.* Some assistance in formulating these plans will often have to be provided by more experienced nations. *American aid should be planned* in consultation with the recipient country *to promote efficiently the country's development plans.* Foreign financial assistance should be carefully geared to the particular social

and economic needs of each society according to the stage it has reached in the development process. In states just beginning to emerge, funds for resource surveys may be all they can absorb. Those at a later stage will need large amounts of capital to broaden their industrial base. The MIT report also suggests that "a substantial portion of [development] capital should . . . be made available in such a way that required repayment in the currency of the lender is to some degree conditional on the degree and pace of the growth process achieved by the borrower."

2) *The importance of long-range commitments of American aid* is difficult to overemphasize. Unless underdeveloped countries can count on receiving continuing assistance from the United States and other donor nations, they cannot make effective long-range plans for their economic growth. It is therefore vital that the United States operate its economic assistance program, first, to establish the principle that aid to underdeveloped countries will be given continuously for the foreseeable future, and, second, to make specific financial commitments for a number of years ahead so that the states can confidently plan on outside aid in mapping their development programs.

3) In addition to the need for capital, the reports stress the *importance of the American technical assistance program*. Technical assistance is much less expensive than the granting of capital, yet it can play a vital role in the development process. The reports urge that the United States broaden its technical assistance program and gear it to the particular needs of each state. U.S. technical assistance should have these five aims: a) To develop to the fullest the human resources of the recipient country by carefully thought-out educational programs which will teach the particular skills needed in the country but will not create a class of educated unemployables; b) to offer opportunities for many groups in the society, not just the urban elite, to participate in the modernization process (e.g., by fostering agricultural extension programs); c) to help create the laws and institutions required by an industrial society (e.g., labor legislation, taxation, social security systems); d) to adapt modern skills and technology to the physical, social, cultural, and economic conditions in the recipient country; e) to convey an image of U.S. purposes and modes of operation which will lay an effective basis for future cooperation.

4) The MIT, Maxwell, and Northwestern studies urge that the *United States strongly support land reform programs*. MIT points to the critical role of such programs in the modernization process and suggests that the United States not only provide the capital to make such programs feasible but also make available the technical assistance and food surpluses necessary to cushion the temporary effects on the economy of agricultural reorganization.

5) More thought and resources should be devoted to fostering native *private enterprise and foreign private investment in underdeveloped areas.* The U.S. aid program must not overlook the foreign exchange needs of small-scale private trade and business in these countries. MIT feels these require-

5

ments might be met by supplying foreign exchange to development banks or other financial institutions in the recipient country, which can then make them available to qualified entrepreneurs locally. The CEIR report suggests encouraging U.S. firms to establish affiliates, under business ownership and management, with funds borrowed from the Development Loan Fund but secured by the affiliate property to minimize private risk. The investment guarantee program of the International Cooperation Administration should also be expanded.

6) *Regional development programs should be encouraged* wherever feasible. The United States must recognize, however, that many underdeveloped countries are too militantly nationalistic to be ready yet for regional cooperation, and it would be unrealistic to make aid programs contingent on regional cooperation. The Conlon report does feel that within the next decade Asia might be ready for a regional development bank administered by Asians and financed by the United States, Western Europe, and Japan.

7) *The need for coordinating American aid programs with the programs of other nations and of the United Nations* is emphasized by the reports. In order to achieve the requisite coordination, most of the reports (except the MIT study) recommend that U.S. and other aid should be channeled increasingly (though not exclusively) through multinational organizations. A multilateral approach to aid would have the additional advantage of enabling economic problems to be tackled on their merits without wounding sensibilities among the recipients or raising fears about intervention in their domestic affairs. This would be particularly important in the sensitive tasks of creating new administrative structures and training the administrative personnel badly needed in emerging nations. Channelling U.S. aid through the U.N. would also discredit any suspicion that the United States wishes to substitute a new imperialism for European colonialism.

The advocates of a predominantly multilateral approach to aid emphasize in particular the need for increased U.S. appropriations to the various U.N. development agencies and the affiliated institutions, such as the World Bank. The Maxwell report goes farther than this and advocates the creation of a development authority under U.N. auspices to coordinate all international development operations. The new authority would define general objectives and operating principles for all the international development programs and would have under it in each country a strong field director to coordinate the local operations of the existing specialized international agencies. Each country director also would have the important task of working out with the local authorities a realistic national development program for the country and would recommend which projects or types of projects should be given priority in the allocation of international funds.

The MIT report strongly opposes the creation of such a global development authority. It insists that "to attempt to lump the existing [national and

6

international] agencies together into a single international organization to administer aid would be neither a feasible nor a desirable solution." MIT's reasons are: a) it is doubtful that with such a system parliamentary bodies of lending nations would make sufficient aid available; b) donor countries may not have the same objectives in giving aid and may try to control administration of their own donated funds; c) new international institutions tend to be created without the old ones being abolished.

The MIT report, like all the other reports, does stress the need for coordinating the efforts of all the national and international agencies offering economic assistance. To accomplish this, three reports (CEIR, FPRI, MIT) urge the formulation of a common Western strategy toward the under-developed countries, with each Western nation fitting its own program, insofar as practicable, into the general strategic plan. Studies should be made to devise such a strategy, and institutions should be created to effect continuing coordination of Western programs.

The importance of American economic aid to the development of emerging nations should not be underestimated, but money alone is not the answer. To carry its fullest possible weight, U.S. aid must be provided discriminately, must be coordinated with that of other nations, and must be given in concert with other facets of American diplomacy.

Trade Policy and U.S. Balance of Payments Deficit

The underdeveloped countries need not only aid but trade. Indeed, according to the FPRI report, "the strengthening and broadening of the West's trade ties with Asia, Africa, and Latin America will probably prove more important than foreign assistance programs in contributing to the economic development of those regions." If trade with these areas is restricted, their growth may be so inhibited that they will find it difficult to repay U.S. loans or they may feel forced to trade increasingly with the Communist bloc.

There are other reasons why it is important for the United States to foster international trade: expanded trade stimulates our own internal growth, promotes our international political influence, and strengthens the economies of the industrial nations of the West.

Many pressures are building up for the United States to adopt restrictionist trade policies. Our imports are rising as we become increasingly dependent on foreign ores, minerals, petroleum, and other materials. Our exports are meeting increasing competition abroad from Western Europe and Japan and will soon begin to encounter competition from the now underdeveloped areas. The U.S. balance of payments deficit is of growing concern.

The reports emphatically agree, however, that the United States should meet these problems *not* by adopting protectionist trade policies, but by pursuing a vigorous program for the expansion of U.S. exports. In its efforts to solve the balance of payments problem, the United States also should neither resort to cutting its economic assistance program nor to following a "tied-loan policy" (i.e., one requiring countries to use U.S. aid funds to purchase U.S. goods). Instead, the U.S. government and U.S. business should take new actions to increase U.S. exports, and the United States should work to lessen trade restrictions throughout the free world. As the underdeveloped countries progress, they will provide increased competition for U.S. goods, but they will also open up enlarged markets for U.S. exports. These countries will be able to afford our exports only if their imports can be absorbed by the United States and Western Europe.

Diplomatic Policy

For an effective diplomatic policy toward the underdeveloped nations, the reports emphasize that the United States must recognize the forces which have led these states to seek a policy of neutrality between East and West. America should not seek to alter this stance or to force states into military alliances. On the contrary, the United States should recognize that neutrality may be the best path for many of these countries to follow in seeking their economic development. Our national interests in the long range will be better served by helping to build stable, strong, independent countries than by depending on weak, unstable military allies.

The United States must also accept the fact that in many of the underdeveloped states it will be impossible to sustain wholly democratic governments in the early stages of development. We must be prepared to work with leaders who, while genuinely committed to the ultimate institution of democratic systems, nevertheless find it impossible to work within democratic forms for the present. U.S. aid and other programs, however, should be designed to foster in the long run a political and social climate favorable to democracy. That this ultimate democracy can take many different forms must be understood by the United States.

The rising tide of nationalism in the underdeveloped countries is a force that merits U.S. sympathy and understanding even when it conflicts with the policies of U.S. allies who are colonial powers. To some extent we can balance our commitments to our allies and our sympathy with the emerging nations by encouraging progressive European policies toward colonies and by supporting the development of new political relationships such as the Commonwealth of Nations and the French Community. To avoid being tarred with the colonial brush, the United States, according to the Maxwell report, should not give aid to countries still in a colonial status and should concentrate its assistance programs in countries already independent.

The need is stressed for the United States to establish contacts in depth with the underdeveloped areas: that is, to *maintain relations not only with the governments in power but with potential ruling groups* and other emerging

8

interests within the underdeveloped societies. Not only U.S. officials but also non-government personnel (e.g., U.S. businessmen, missionaries, journalists) should have broader contacts in foreign countries.

In addition to seeking to develop friendly relations with all emerging nations, the United States should use its good offices to try to settle disputes between them. Where appropriate, we should offer economic aid to ease particular conflicts (as we did in the Indus Valley dispute between Pakistan and India), and we should always try to isolate these disputes from the cold war. The United States should not only try to mitigate differences between these countries but should also promote active cooperation between them. Regional cooperation can bring many advantages to the underdeveloped areas. Leadership in regional cooperation in Asia can best be supplied by India and Japan because of their technical lead and industrial production.

Military Policy

The problem of military defense of underdeveloped areas against Sino-Soviet aggression is an important one and should not be lost sight of in concentration on the need to contribute to the modernization of these countries. Nevertheless, the formation of military alliances may not be the most effective way of defending these countries against aggression. Whatever contribution they may make to joint Western defense, these alliances and the rearmament they bring about in neighboring countries have a serious detrimental effect on economic growth. In addition, efforts by the United States to bring countries into alliances have had grave political repercussions throughout Asia and the Middle East. Finally, emphasis on the problem of direct aggression fails to consider the fact that subversion and other forms of indirect aggression are probably the most serious Communist threats to the independence of underdeveloped countries.

Yet military leaders have played a dominant role in the development of many new states and have generally exerted an anti-Communist influence. It is important that the United States continue to cultivate the friendship and support of these groups. The Conlon and MIT reports also recommend U.S. encouragement of officer training programs which will provide these military men with the administrative and managerial skills necessary in the new tasks they are assuming as guarantors of stability in some underdeveloped nations.

Information Policy

According to the Conlon report, American information programs toward the underdeveloped areas should put less emphasis on U.S. material prosperity and more emphasis on U.S. dynamism, creativity, desire for peace, and sympathy with the development goals of the new states. MIT asserts that our information program should stress data on technical, political, and other aspects of the modernization process. We must remember, however, that the battle for men's minds being fought in the underdeveloped countries will be won mainly on the basis of American action throughout the world, and not on the basis of information programs within particular countries.

Problems of Specific Areas

India and Pakistan

The critical role of India in the process of economic development in Africa, Asia, the Middle East, and Latin America is difficult to overestimate. As the MIT study puts it:

> In the coming decade India may experience either a decisive break-through to modernization under democratic auspices and an association with the West, or a critical failure which would damage, perhaps irrevocably, the prestige of democracy in India, if not in all of Asia. Given the relatively modest sums involved for both the U.S. and Western Europe and the enormous common costs of failure, this is an occasion for boldness and generosity.

Other studies agree and propose that in order to make the maximum contribution possible to the success of Indian development plans, the United States should make a long-range commitment to provide India with needed capital for her economic growth. In particular, we should help meet India's critical need for foreign exchange during her present five-year plan. The Conlon report suggests that the United States might consider negotiating an agreement among India, the United States, the U.S.S.R. and other interested countries for long-term support of given segments of the plan. Another suggestion of the Conlon report is that Congress might pass special legislation for India to meet her particular foreign aid needs.

The MIT study suggests that, in addition to foreign exchange, India should be supplied with food from American surpluses in order to insure that bad harvests do not create major set-backs to Indian development. This would also encourage the Indians to increase employment and domestic purchasing power without excessive worry about inflation. A number of other reports also urge constructive use of American surpluses.

While providing major aid to India, the United States should not ignore the importance of assistance to Pakistan. Even though the reports are agreed that the United States should not seek to bring other countries into military alliances, the United States clearly has an obligation to provide aid to those states which are willing to join it in planning for defense against Communist aggression. However, the United States should encourage Pakistan to cut down the budgetary priority given its military establishment and to devote more concentrated attention to the basic economic problems of the country. As Pakistan develops its plans for economic growth, the U.S. should make contributions equally as generous as those to India.

Japan

Since Japan has become highly industrialized, her need is for trade, not aid. Importing over 80 percent of her industrial raw materials, which she then processes and sells abroad, Japan must find increasing markets in the free world or turn to her former markets on the Chinese mainland. It is not enough that the United States avoid trade restrictions against Japan. The Conlon report recommends that the United States take the lead in exploring what bilateral and multilateral organizations might facilitate U.S.-Japanese economic relations, while Japan herself might continue with vigorous efforts to diversify and expand her exports to the United States and provide a better investment climate in Japan for American firms.

Africa

The entrance into the United Nations of a large number of African states symbolizes the new importance of Africa on the international scene. Until very recently, the United States has failed to give proper attention to Africa in its programs of aid toward underdeveloped areas. The reports stress the need for treating the new African states as a vital sector of the world community, although they are still in the very early stages of development. At this stage, long-range economic development programs are unlikely to emerge in many of the African states.

In this period, therefore, American aid should attempt to lay the groundwork for more rapid economic development in the future, including encouraging planning for development on a regional basis, since many of the African states cannot independently become viable economic units. In addition to urging American aid for economic surveys and other preliminaries to economic development, the reports stress the importance of education on the African scene. African countries are vitally short of professional men and technicians, and the United States should take the lead in providing opportunities for education both within Africa and in the United States and Western Europe for Africans from the new states. Until enough Africans are trained for both technical and administrative positions, the United States should help supply specialists to fill the gap. Several reports stress the need for special preparation for Americans going to work in Africa. The Northwestern study suggests the establishment of an international career service for technical assistance personnel, to be developed in cooperation with other countries, through the United Nations.

The reports urge that U.S. policy should aim to keep Africa insulated from the cold war and to minimize intra-African aggression. The possibility of an arms embargo to Africa should be thoroughly explored. The studies emphasize, too, the influence which American domestic policies, particularly

11

policies toward the American Negro, will have on our relations with Africa. It is important, says the Northwestern study, that American embassies *not* discriminate in their personnel policies, even in those remaining white-settler countries in Africa which do practice discrimination. Furthermore, American businesses in Africa should be encouraged to be more progressive in their employment policies.

Middle East

Under the leadership of the United States, the Western nations should now take the initiative to advance Middle Eastern economic development in ways which will thwart Soviet attempts to capture lucrative markets and will help spark a unified effort toward economic progress among *all* the countries of the area, including Israel. The importance of some sort of regional development institution for the Middle East is stressed by both the Maxwell and the Senate staff reports.

These reports as well as the Harvard Center report warn against too close direct U.S. involvement in Middle Eastern affairs and recommend "discreet economic support." The strength of nationalistic feeling in Arab states demands a development institution run "by the people of the region." Since this nationalism is shaped more by regional than by single nation loyalties, an institution devoted to development of all Arab states is feasible and is in the best interests of the United States.

The Senate staff study on the Middle East makes recommendations for the solution of the Palestine refugee problem, which it calls "the heart of the Arab-Israeli quarrel [and] . . . the major obstacle to stability in the Middle East." The principal recommendations are that Israel should agree not only to reimbursement of the refugees but also to their *right* to repatriation in Israel, while the Arab leaders should agree to accept all refugees who wish to settle in their countries.

N.B.: Detailed discussion of Latin America policy is absent in these reports. "United States-Latin American Relations" was the title of a special series of subcontract studies prepared in 1959-60 for the Subcommittee on American Republics Affairs of the Senate Committee on Foreign Relations. These seven studies are now combined into a single document: Senate Doc. 125, 86th Congress, Second Session; Government Printing Office, Washington, D. C., August 1960.

III. THE COMMUNIST CHALLENGE

The studies agree that the Sino-Soviet threat to the United States is likely to continue. They warn that despite possible changes in Soviet tactics the basic desire for world domination will remain the motivating force of Soviet policy. Thus, conflict between the United States and the Soviet bloc, whether it goes by the name of cold war or "peaceful coexistence", will continue. The alternative to competition between the United States and the Soviet Union can only be acquiescence to the Soviet desire to take over ever greater portions of the earth.

Yet there is general agreement with the observation of the Harvard-Columbia report on the U.S.S.R. and Eastern Europe, that American foreign policy should not be aimed exclusively at containing the Russian threat. With one exception, the studies agree that U.S. policy toward its NATO allies and the uncommitted nations of Africa, Asia, the Middle East, and Latin America should be developed on the basis of consultation with these countries and not merely as a response to Soviet pressures or Soviet successes. The military aspects of this challenge will be considered in a later chapter; here we deal with the other aspects of the Soviet drive for world domination.

The Economic Challenge

The problems posed by Soviet economic growth have received considerable attention in the literature on American foreign policy. As the Harvard-Columbia group notes, it is impossible to be categorical about where the Soviet economy will be ten years from now; but it goes on to say:

> It seems likely that the industrial goals of the Soviet 7-year plan will be met or bettered, while the agricultural goals seem less likely of fulfillment. While it appears doubtful that Mr. Khrushchev can make good his boasts that the Soviet economy will outstrip American production by 1970, his country may be able to validate that boast by a later date. Soviet industrial output may surpass that of the United States in 15 or 20 years. If present trends continue, the Soviet economy as a whole, in spite of a somewhat reduced growth rate from previous years, will, nevertheless, continue to grow perhaps twice as fast as ours.

> But after this assumption has been reached, it is necessary to emphasize that the aggregate figures do not tell the whole story, or even the most important part of it. It is not the prospect of the rising curve of Soviet Gross National Product crossing ours at some future time, whether 1970 or 1980, that creates the main problem for us, although Mr. Khrushchev defines it in these terms. What does create the problem for American foreign policy is the way in which these resources are used or will be used.

Soviet economic growth affects three aspects of Soviet-American relations: 1) the U.S.-U.S.S.R. military balance; 2) the resources available to the U.S.S.R. for conducting its foreign economic policies; and 3) U.S.-U.S.S.R. prestige among underdeveloped areas of the world.

The Maxwell study holds that "since the limiting factor is not steel but brains and will, the prospect of a continued Soviet gain in industrial prowess is not of decisive military importance." The Harvard-Columbia group states that the industrial capacity of the Soviets will remain an important factor in the military equilibrium, and increased Soviet growth coupled with a willingness to continue to spend a large percentage of her Gross National Product for defense, will pose a serious military threat to the United States. Although nuclear weapons may themselves become cheap, hardening and mobility of missiles is very expensive and the achievement of a stable, strategic deterrent will call for the development of large-scale conventional, limited-war forces which again are highly costly in terms of industrial capacity. Finally, the size of a country's Gross National Product has a strong bearing on the amount of money which it can afford to devote to research and development, which the Maxwell study recognizes as likely to be the critical area of the arms race.

The Harvard-Columbia study also warns of the increased dangers resulting from a stepped-up Soviet foreign economic offensive. As the Soviet economy grows, the willingness of its leaders to use economic means for the advancement of political ends and control of all the apparatus of the economy within the state will put in the hands of the Soviets a major economic tool. With the advantage of a centrally directed economy and the ability to coordinate and turn on and off at will military, political, trade and economic assistance pressures, the Soviet Union will be in a position to use on a much larger scale the same techniques which it has applied from time to time with great effectiveness in the recent past. While the United States is seeking to prevent all countries from entering the Soviet orbit and must therefore give economic aid to a large number of nations, the Soviets can, by concentrating their aid, place a few countries in positions of economic dependence upon the Soviet Union.

The third major danger to the United States posed by the increased growth of the Soviet Union (and China) is the importance of the Communist system as a symbol of economic success to the underdeveloped areas of the world. The Harvard-Columbia study warns that the impact of the image of the Soviet Union as a country which has succeeded in solving the problems of economic development may be the principal political consequence of the growth of the Soviet economy.

This analysis of the problems posed by the increased economic growth of the Communist bloc highlights the importance of a greater growth rate for the United States, and this is emphasized in a number of reports. The CEIR report stresses that our government should take action to stimulate economic productivity. To this end Congress should reappraise existing laws with a view to strengthening incentives for increased savings and eliminating policies which inhibit growth by discouraging savings, restricting capital investment, boosting costs, limiting foreign trade, and imposing unnecessary rigidities on the economy.

Yet, neither in our domestic nor our foreign policies should we be distracted by undue attention to the Soviet threat. In the long run, the most effective check on the Soviet economic offensive will be the development of viable economic and political structures throughout the free world and particularly in the underdeveloped areas.

Negotiating with the Soviets

The studies agree that the U.S. must be continually prepared to negotiate with the Soviet Union on outstanding political problems and disarmament. According to the Council on Foreign Relations, this should preferably be done through normal diplomatic channels rather than through "public performances of ministers or heads of governments." The Harvard-Columbia study points out that America must be prepared to negotiate not only because of the remote possibility of a Soviet change of attitude but because we must make it clear to the people of the non-Communist world where the responsibilty rests for the continuation of the cold war. The study emphasizes, however, the need for an informed and sophisticated public, so that our representatives will not feel pressed to surrender vital positions in order to satisfy public demands for agreement. It also stresses the importance of being ever mindful of the danger of undermining the confidence of our allies by bilateral agreements with the Communist world.

After a brief review of the outstanding territorial and other political issues between the United States and the Soviet Union, the Harvard-Columbia study concludes that there are areas of limited common interests which may make negotiations possible. But it warns that it is unreal to anticipate that

the process of negotiation can in the near future dissolve the central and decisive issues which lie at the heart of the struggle. We are obliged to take at face value Mr. Khrushchev's reminders that a period of peaceful coexistence in Soviet policy does not imply a suspension of the Soviet commitment to its long-term vision of a Communist world. At the same time, we must as a people have the maturity to make it possible to be resolute about resisting future Soviet expansion at the same time that we are continuously open to the diplomatic exploration of the possibilities for settlement.

Other studies agree that direct transactions with the Soviet Union cannot change the fundamental conflict between the American and Soviet systems, but that the United States must remain ready to seek through negotiation the settlement of particular problems between the Soviet Union and the non-Communist world, and at the same time be prepared to take advantage of contradictions and errors in Soviet actions and policies.

On Germany, the Harvard-Columbia study declares that the United States must continue to guarantee the independence of West Berlin, and, though it must recognize the difficulty of achieving the unification of Germany, it must not give formal sanction to the present division. This study rejects, as does the FPRI study, any of the suggested proposals for disengagement in Europe.

The Harvard-Columbia study further urges that the United States explore the possible mutual interests of the U.S.S.R. and the United States in preventing the outbreak of war in the Middle East, Asia and the Far East. It suggests specifically that the United States and the Soviet Union might be interested in preventing explosions in such places as Formosa, Vietnam, and the Chinese-Indian border.

Internal Changes in the Soviet Union

An important question for U.S. policy is whether the United States may anticipate changes in the character of Soviet foreign policy objectives as a result of internal changes within the Soviet world. The Harvard-Columbia study warns against believing that the development of the Soviet economy in the near future will produce a new middle class of managerial and technical personnel which will have a decisive effect on Soviet foreign policy goals. While development of Soviet society may lead it to be less arbitrary, less totalitarian and increasingly stable, there is no reason to believe that this process of evolution will be accompanied by a normalization of Soviet relations with the rest of the world.

The Harvard-Columbia study agrees with the Harvard Center study that in the immediate future there is likely to be an erosion of ideological commitment with respect to the domestic policies of the Soviet Union. But again, it warns against the belief that the erosion of internal ideology will lead to a dropping of the Soviet commitment to the domination of the world. Rather it argues that the principal determinant of the Soviet goals will be its future successes in expanding the domains of Communism. The United States should limit its concern with Soviet behavior to international situations and not attempt to alter the internal organization of the Soviet Union.

Communist Bloc Relations

The Harvard-Columbia and the Harvard Center studies agree that the Communist bloc is likely to face continuing internal differences over the next decades and the Soviet Union will find it increasingly hard to assert unquestioned leadership. But they warn that this erosion of Russian hegemony is at best a long-range prospect, and no hopeful results for American policy should be expected in the near future.

16

The cohesive effect of Communist ideology plus the latent threat of Soviet force will probably preserve Soviet domination over Eastern Europe for the next decade even if Soviet troops should be withdrawn from these countries. The studies urge, however, that the United States continue to keep open channels of communication with the peoples of Eastern Europe. We should express concern for the welfare of these peoples and should pursue a policy of the broadest and deepest possible contact with them through cultural, economic and other exchanges.

The FPRI study is optimistic about the possibilities of affecting conditions in the Eastern European satellites, calling them "the most potent force of anti-Communism and anti-Russianism in the world today". It agrees with the other studies that the West must support by every possible peaceful means the right of self-determination for these people. Nevertheless, the Harvard Center and the Harvard-Columbia studies warn against assuming that the liberation of these areas is in any sense imminent. They suggest rather that America maintain the necessary contacts with the existing governments while attempting to keep alive the hope of ultimate liberation of these countries.

Relations between the U.S.S.R. and China, which will increasingly become those of partners, pose the most serious challenge to the unity of the Communist bloc. However, the studies commenting on Sino-Soviet relations (Conlon, Harvard Center, and Harvard-Colombia) all hold that the Sino-Soviet alliance is based on mutual interests which outweigh present negative factors. The studies, therefore, argue against basing American policy on the assumption of an early split between Communist China and Russia, although the possibility should not be ruled out that Soviet policy in the near future may be influenced by its long-range estimates of the dangers of Communist China. Efforts to break up the alliance, the Harvard Center study adds, may only serve to drive China and Russia closer together.

The Problem of China

The problem of China is not whether China should be allowed to participate in the world scene. She is already doing so, economically, politically, and militarily, and, as her industrial capacity grows, her influence, particulary throughout Asia, will increase.

In these circumstances, the Maxwell study points out "the central issue of American policy has practically nothing to do with the hotly debated question of recognizing the Communist regime and admitting it to the United Nations. The central issue is . . . how can the U.S. best act to contain the Communist threat to the free nations of Asia." The Maxwell report recommends that America give primary emphasis to the development of strong, free societies in the Asian countries, and that it not seek to deal with the Communist Chinese challenge directly.

17

On the other hand, the Conlon study suggests that, working in carefully thought out stages, America should proceed slowly to investigate the possibilities for normalizing the relations with Communist China; this should be done, however, in a way that would permit the continued existence on Taiwan of an independent government. The Conlon report holds that this policy might not only serve to stabilize the situation in the Far East, but that it is necessary if the U.S. is to maintain the support of its allies on its Chinese policy.

IV. THE MILITARY CHALLENGE: DETERRENCE, DEFENSE, AND ARMS CONTROL

All of the studies which deal with military problems agree that the American defense effort is inadequate. Given the present military threat to the security of the United States, America has been living too dangerously. The spending of additional money, which it could well afford, would result in much greater assurance that it would suffer neither total destruction nor defeat in local aggression because of the inadequacy of its military preparations.

There is no disagreement in the studies on what the goals of American military policy should be. These goals are the prevention of war, the limiting of damage should war occur, and the providing of a military umbrella under which other forms of foreign policy can be carried out. In other words, American military policy must be aimed not only at preventing a military attack directly on the United States, but also at preventing the Communists from taking over areas vital to the security of the United States. The Johns Hopkins study on military policy notes that both deterrence and arms control are appropriate means to these military goals.

The Strategic Balance

Until fairly recently American policy makers have assumed that the strategic balance between the United States and the Soviet Union was somehow inherently stable. The phrase "the balance of terror" summed up the notion that with the existence of thermonuclear weapons neither the United States nor the Soviet Union could ever launch an all-out nuclear attack on the other without the certainty of retaliation in kind. However, as has become evident in recent years and as the Johns Hopkins study stresses, this is by no means the case. Maintaining the stability of the strategic balance requires on the part of the United States the development of effective, invulnerable, strategic weapons systems and a continued program of research and development.

The great concern expressed about the stability of the strategic balance results from an increased understanding of the problems of vulnerability. Until recently American leaders tended to measure the American strategic force in terms of the blow it was capable of delivering on the Soviet Union with its existing force level. This analysis ignored the fact that the United States was committed to accepting a strike from the Soviet Union before retaliating. A Soviet strike is almost certain to concentrate on destroying the American strategic force, its SAC bases, and its ballistic missile sites. It is only those elements that manage to survive a Soviet surprise attack which, in fact, would be capable of retaliating against the Soviet Union. Thus, adequate American strategic power to deter a Soviet strike rests not on the force in being prior to the strike but on that part of the force which is capable of surviving a Soviet attack and delivering an unacceptable amount of damage on the Soviet Union, following a well coordinated Soviet surprise strike upon the United States.

With the Soviet development of operational intercontinental ballistic missiles (ICBM's) the problem of developing an invulnerable American strategic force has been greatly complicated. America now needs a force which could survive a strike by missiles giving virtually no warning and carrying powerful warheads to within a maximum of 2 miles of their designated targets. The present American SAC bases could not hope to survive a Soviet missile strike, nor could the present missiles being built in the United States and being placed overseas on allied bases. Such sites are soft, that is, they could be destroyed by a relatively small warhead landing only approximately close to the target at which it is aimed.

Invulnerability, the Johns Hopkins study points out, depends on either mobility or hardness. The American striking force must be constantly on the move, or it must be hardened (that is, physically sheltered, usually in underground reinforced shelters) so that only a very accurate strike requiring more than one missile could destroy it. But the problem of developing an invulnerable strategic force is not simply the problem of protecting the weapons themselves. In addition, the United States must make invulnerable its communications and control systems, and at the same time devise means to protect the leaders who must order the weapons to be launched. The problem is extraordinarily complex and can be met only if the notion of the need for an invulnerable force is explicitly accepted and if there is a willingness to spend significantly larger sums than are now being spent.

In developing strategic forces, it is not only necessary to insure their invulnerability against Russian surprise attack, but it is necessary to determine for what missions the forces are expected to be used. In general, the missions for strategic forces are two: 1) to destroy the strategic striking power of the enemy, and 2) to destroy his cities. American deterrence of the Soviet strategic attack depends, as the Council on Foreign Relations notes, on the ability to inflict unacceptable damage upon the Soviet Union, that is, the ability to destroy cities and industrial power. While urging the United States to rely primarily on a force capable of inflicting overwhelming damage on Soviet industrial complexes, the Johns Hopkins study suggests that some counterforce capacity be continued capable of rational target selection in a retaliatory strike.

The difficulties of maintaining an effective, invulnerable deterrent to a Soviet strategic strike are compounded by the complexities of research and development and the problem of lead time. The strategic balance at any given time is predicated on the assumption that neither side will make a significant technological breakthrough. But if, for example, either side were to develop a truly effective anti-ICBM system, the strategic balance would be radically altered. It is therefore necessary for the United States to maintain vigorous research and development programs in order to keep up with the Soviet Union and prevent the possibility of a Soviet breakthrough which would seriously undermine American security. The problem of lead time makes it necessary for American research and development to be carried on imaginatively, for the strategic balance as it exists today was shaped by procurement decisions taken four, five or more years ago. Only in limited ways can the United States now alter the strategic balance for the early 1960's. It is on the basis of decisions taken now in research and procurement that American security in the middle and late sixties will depend. Thus, even an Administration concerned about the present inadequacy of our strategic system could not hope to make significant alterations immediately.

In light of this analysis, the nature of the missile gap facing the United States becomes clear. The missile gap period which, according to the Johns Hopkins study, the United States is about to enter, will be a phase during which the Soviet Union will have a decisive advantage over the United States in the strategic arena and when, unless vigorous action is taken, the Soviet Union will have the ability to destroy the American strategic force.

A number of means to reduce or possibly to prevent this Soviet military advantage are available. They include a greater dispersal of SAC bombers, the placing of a number of aircraft on high alert status, and other protective expedients. These measures cannot guarantee the preservation of our present strategic power into the early 1960's, but they may at least prevent the achievement of decisive first strike advantage by the enemy.

For long-term strengthening of the U.S. strategic position, the Johns Hopkins study makes a number of specific proposals. In general it urges that the United States assign top priority to reducing the vulnerability of American strategic forces and that this be done by increasing the mobility, concealment, hardening and dispersal of bases, communications and warning systems, control centers, and missile launching sites and personnel. Increased research and development efforts should be directed toward the manufacture of improved delivery and guidance systems for intercontinental ballistic missiles. The study also advocates that the United States accelerate the development of solid fuel ICBM's capable of mobility and hardening.

The United States should not rely on a single strategic system, but should develop a diversified system. Any one strategic system, for example the Polaris submarine, is subject to the dangers of a breakthrough by the Soviet Union which would render what now appears to be an invulnerable system highly vulnerable. To achieve a stable, invulnerable strategic system requires the United States to develop a diversified system based on hardening and mobility not only of weapons themselves but of their control and command systems.

21

Defense of Local Areas

In addition to deterring a strategic strike upon America, the United States is committed to the defense of local areas against Communist aggression. All of the studies assert that the United States must uphold its commitments to defend these areas against Communist aggression. The studies urge that the United States be prepared to defend local areas, not by the use of its strategic fighting force or the threat of the use of this force, but by using indigenous and allied ground forces. No study contradicted, and many echoed, the assertion made by the Johns Hopkins group that the United States must adopt a policy of limited war for the defense of local areas.

The studies dealing with the question of the role of nuclear weapons in limited war (the Johns Hopkins and FPRI studies) were agreed on what American policy should be. While the United States and its allies must develop forces capable of using tactical nuclear weapons in the event that the Russians should attack using such weapons, the studies stress the importance of maintaining the capability for fighting conventionally. The Johns Hopkins study argues that the notion that the use of nuclear weapons would make up for any numerical advantage of troops that the enemy might have is simply erroneous. America would suffer grave political costs should it initiate the use of nuclear weapons in a limited war. For both political and military reasons, the United States should base its defense of local areas on its ability to move conventional forces quickly into such areas to stem aggression before it has a chance to spread.

The Johns Hopkins study further points out that, if both the United States and the Soviet Union develop stable strategic systems in the late 1960's, the danger of limited war is likely to increase. In part, at least, the deterrence of limited war up to now has been the fear of such a war spiralling into total war because of the instabilities of the strategic balance discussed above. When the strategic balance becomes stable, either because of the unilateral action of both sides or because of arms control agreements, the danger of limited war and hence the need for powerful, mobile American ground forces will greatly increase.

Problems of the NATO Alliance

The NATO alliance poses particular military, as well as diplomatic, problems. The FPRI study argues that the United States help to develop in Western Europe a comprehensive military posture aimed at deterring both total and limited war. In addition, it stresses the importance of building up the political cohesion of NATO as a vital prerequisite for its continued functioning as an effective military alliance. To increase the limited war capability of the NATO forces, it urges that at least one additional American division be placed on the European continent assigned to the NATO alliance. NATO forces should be better equipped, both for conventional and nuclear war, but they should be prepared to defend Western Europe at the conventional level unless the Soviets initiate the use of nuclear weapons.

One of the few major disagreements in the reports involves the question of whether NATO should develop its own strategic striking force to deter Soviet aggression. The FPRI study urges that the United States contribute to the development of a strategic force under the control of the NATO alliance; it suggests that such a force is necessary for the defense of Europe to prevent successful Soviet blackmail of the NATO countries. The Johns Hopkins study, on the other hand, argues that "because independent allied strategic forces can add little to the deterrence supplied by the U.S. strategic forces and because they tend to divert allied efforts from more pressing needs of local defense, the United States should discourage the establishment or extension of independent, nuclear forces." The two studies agree, however, that if the Allied countries are determined to proceed with the development of strategic forces, the United States should provide technical assistance in order to avoid costly duplication of effort. They also agree that the only possibility of an effective NATO system would be one based on mobile missiles.

Arms Control

The Johns Hopkins and Council on Foreign Relations studies declare that America must take seriously its commitment to a policy of arms control. The Johns Hopkins study suggests that arms control is really one of several aspects of America's national security strategy aimed at maximizing its military security in the nuclear missile age. This study cautions against accepting complete disarmament, which would have many pitfalls. It urges, however, that the United States seriously pursue limited arms control arrangements which could contemplate the maintenance of sizable forces on both the Allied and the Russian sides. The Johns Hopkins study further points out that many arms control policies can be put into effect unilaterally, that is, the United States could take steps to harden its strategic forces to make them look less menacing to the Soviet Union and to reduce the present significant dangers of accidental war without coming to an agreement with the Soviet Union. Such measures might contribute to the stability of the strategic balance without weakening America's military posture.

Although much can be done unilaterally, the Johns Hopkins study also points out that certain problem areas, such as the spread of strategic nuclear weapons to additional countries, probably require formal agreements backed by realistic control and inspection. But such problem areas, the Council on Foreign Relations study suggests, must be examined, not in the abstract, but in relation to the dangers of the present arms race and strategic balance. If an arms control proposal promises greater stability and a reduced danger of war, it might be worth accepting, even though 100 per cent foolproof inspection would be impossible.

Finally, the studies are agreed on the need for much greater research on heretofore sadly neglected technical and strategic problems of arms control. Although the studies are not over-optimistic about the possibility of reaching control agreements with the Soviet Union, they argue that the stakes are so high that the United States cannot afford to leave unreviewed any possibilities for ending the present nuclear arms race.

V. INSTRUMENTS OF U.S. FOREIGN POLICY

Effective American foreign policy, the studies agree, depends most on intelligent policies and vigorous leadership. Nevertheless, changes in the machinery of foreign-policy making and execution could have an important influence on the success of American policy in the world. Effective structures cannot guarantee successful foreign policy, but poor structures can interfere even with the most vigorous and intelligent policy. It is with this recognition of the significant, though limited, role of structural change that the studies outline a number of specific recommendations.

The National Security Policy Process

The Brookings Institution study suggests that the national security policy process cannot and should not be centered in the National Security Council. The Council provides a specialized, high-level forum for coordinating consideration by key department heads of major foreign policy issues. But this is clearly not enough, and the Brookings Institution study concludes that "most of the hard thinking in this field must be done outside rather than inside the Council." The study urges that the NSC should concentrate not on formal and routine discussion of a number of issues, but rather on the imaginative and informal analysis of major foreign policy problems facing the country.

In particular, it suggests that a determined effort be made to coordinate substantive with budgetary considerations so that the NSC, in considering proposals, is clear on the relationship between them and the budget currently being prepared by the Budget Bureau in consultation with the various departments.

The Role of the Department of State

The Brookings and Maxwell studies agree that there should be a single officer in charge of coordinating all aspects of American foreign policy, including, the Maxwell study notes, "such difficult cases as the Defense Department, the budgeting process, and tariff and loan policy." Both studies also urge the development of a foreign policy planning staff able to carry on comprehensive long-range planning comparable to the long-range planning now done for military operations.

The studies disagree, however, on the major proposal made in the Brookings study: the creation of a new post of Secretary of Foreign Affairs. The Brookings study proposes that a new Department of Foreign Affairs be created to promote unified responsibility for foreign policy planning and that this department have three under-departments, the Department of State, the Department of Foreign Economic Operations, and the Department of Information and Cultural Affairs. Under this scheme, the Secretary of State would be responsible only for the strictly political aspects of American foreign policy and for negotiating with and visiting foreign countries, while the new Secretary of Foreign Affairs would concentrate on the development and execution of policy embracing military, economic, and public information as well as political aspects.

The Maxwell study, on the other hand, argues that the functions of coordination should be placed in the hands of the existing Secretary of State. It holds that the man seeking to perform this coordinating function must have roots in a single operating department and objects to the Brookings proposal to put the U.S. Information Agency and the International Cooperation Administration in a common agency with the present State Department. It urges that everything possible be done to enhance the competence and prestige of the Secretary of State and proposes considering making him the Executive Vice-Chairman of the NSC.

The Coordination of Foreign and Military Policy Making

The Brookings study points out that it is impossible to plan rational foreign and military policy separately. They interact closely and must reinforce each other in vital ways. However, in practice, foreign policy and military policy have frequently been uncoordinated and in some cases conflicting. The Brookings and Maxwell studies suggest that the Secretary of State should play an important role in the formation of military policy and in determining budget levels for defense spending. To provide the Secretary of State with the necessary understanding of military problems he requires a staff, civilian or military, who are familiar with military strategy and can furnish him with independent advice on these problems.

It is also important for regular career foreign service officers to have a greater awareness of military strategy problems, and for career military officers to have an understanding of the political factors which affect military policy. The Brookings study urges increased attendance at military staff colleges by foreign policy specialists and increased personnel exchanges between military and civilian agencies.

The Secretary of Defense, moreover, should assume the role of a military strategist rather than of just a manager of the defense establishment. The Brookings study urges that increased use be made of the Office of International Security Affairs to provide the Secretary of Defense with background on political factors. Although both the Secretary of Defense and the Secretary of State should thus be men who have a clear grasp of political and military problems and the interrelationship between them, and both should play an active role in the shaping of overall policy, the primary role of coordination should rest with the Secretary of State.

Field Operations

The MIT study joins with the Brookings and Maxwell studies in urging that increased power be given to the ambassador for the coordination of overseas operations. The studies recognize the importance of giving initiative for day-to-day operations to program administrators in the field, but they also point out the necessity of coordinating America's economic, political, military and public information policies in each country. This function the ambassador should fulfill.

The Brookings study emphasizes the importance of having fully qualified ambassadors, if the ambassador's role is to be expanded in this way. It suggests that in the future the skills needed by the ambassador are more likely to be developed in career officials than in non-career appointees. Nevertheless, it argues that the position of the chief of the mission is of such vital importance that it should be filled by the most highly qualified individual, whether career or non-career. Certainly, the study declares, "the inadequacy of governmental allowances should never be a determining factor in the appointment of an ambassador."

Foreign Service Problems

The Brookings study urges the State Department to develop policies to increase flexibility in career patterns as a means of promoting special as well as general skills among career officers. It proposes separate examinations to facilitate the recruitment of specialists. The importance of language skills for American representatives abroad is widely stressed in the studies, which applaud the recent State Department efforts to improve the language ability of its officials and urge that the programs be supported by increased Congressional appropriations.

Congressional Structures

Congressional involvement in foreign affairs has grown steadily in the post-war period. This has been a result not only of increased American involvement abroad, but also of the fact that more and more aspects of what was once solely domestic policy now have a direct impact on foreign relations. Policies relating to economic growth, trade, agriculture, credit and so on, all have important effects on America's diplomatic standing in the world.

Even subjects with no direct relationship to foreign affairs can have important bearings on the success of American policy. The studies on Africa and Asia point out, for example, that the policy of the United States Government towards the treatment of American Negroes is of great significance in relations with the underdeveloped areas of the world. As the Brookings study points out, more than half of the standing committees of Congress today deal regularly with issues of international significance.

The Brookings study emphasizes, therefore, the importance of coordinating Congressional action on foreign policy matters. It suggests that Congress consider the creation of a new joint select committee to study national security problems; this new committee would bring together the chairmen and the ranking minority members of the principal committees involved in international problems. Alternatively, the Brookings study proposes that the two foreign policy committees conduct periodic investigations of American national security policy, inviting participation by leading members of other committees. It advocates expansion of the staffs of committees dealing with foreign policy problems and of the foreign policy research section of the Legislative Reference Service.

The Brookings study points out particularly the importance of greater coordination between the appropriations and substantive committees on foreign policy matters in order to relate individual appropriations to broad policy aims and to eliminate overlapping research and review. It suggests that appropriations be put on a multi-year basis, especially for foreign aid operations, with accompanying annual Congressional review.

Multilateral Instruments

The importance of active U.S. support for the United Nations is underlined by the reports. We should help to strengthen the United Nations by using its present facilities when they serve the objectives we believe in and by exploring possible new responsibilities for the organization. It is not inconceivable that the United Nations could play a significant role in supervising some future agreement on the limitation and control of arms. It might also develop a permanent mobile military force for dealing with local trouble spots. The United States should make more effective use of the judicial organ of the United Nations, the International Court of Justice. If and when enlargement of the United Nations Security Council is contemplated, the Conlon report feels the United States should work for the inclusion of India and Japan on the Council.

The United States should continue to support the development of a European Common Market, provided that present institutions of European economic unity are not multiplied and transformed, in the words of the FPRI study, into "instruments of discrimination against other members of the Atlantic Community". The dramatic economic recovery of Western Europe has led to increased competition of European goods for U.S. markets both domestic and foreign. The United States now has an obligation to protect its own international economic position by urging that the tariffs erected around Common Market nations do not generally exceed the tariffs which now prevail with the separate nations, and by entering into reciprocal trade agreements with the Common Market as a single entity.

SUMMARY OUTLINES OF THE
13 SENATE REPORTS

Study No. 1

WORLDWIDE AND DOMESTIC ECONOMIC PROBLEMS AND THEIR IMPACT ON THE FOREIGN POLICY OF THE UNITED STATES

Corporation for Economic and
Industrial Research, Inc.
Jefferson Davis Highway
Arlington, Virginia

Published: August 1959

GOALS OF THE REPORT

1. *To determine* the major economic problems which will affect U.S. foreign policy during the next decade.
2. *To recommend* possible solutions to these long-range problems. These solutions must deal with the need:
   a. To formulate foreign and domestic policies which can promote economic growth together with financial stability.
   b. To further policies which strengthen the economic positions of allied developed countries.
   c. To liberalize international trade to promote free world strength.
   d. To develop free world cooperative programs to assist underdeveloped areas in achieving economic systems which foster growth along with increased availability of consumer goods ("growth with consumption").
   e. To devise economic policies which cope with:
      (1) the rapid rate of economic and industrial growth of the Soviet Union and
      (2) Soviet determination to win underdeveloped areas and the entire world to communism.

MAJOR PREMISES OF THE REPORT

1. Economic growth is neither inevitable nor automatic.
2. To meet the requirements of adequate defense and successful foreign policies, the U.S. government must concern itself with programs to promote economic growth.
3. Policies to maintain foreign confidence in the dollar constitute a major task for the U.S. government.
4. The Soviets' unremitting ambition to control the world is the fundamental fact underlying U.S. foreign policy problems.
5. The coming decade will see no abatement in the cold war or in the military burdens it imposes on the U.S. economy.
6. The free world currently possesses an overwhelming economic advantage over Communist countries. The advantage can be maintained.
7. The U.S., in concert with the rest of the free world, must meet the growing requirements of the underdeveloped world. The principal instruments for meeting these requirements are foreign aid programs and the fostering of international trade.

I. PROBLEMS OF ECONOMIC GROWTH IN MAJOR WORLD AREAS.

A. U.S.S.R. AND THE U.S.

1. Problems of economic growth are not simply a set of problems in pure economics; they are also tempered by the challenges of foreign and defense policy. U.S. growth occurs without the comprehensive and unified programming for capital accumulation and allocation available to Soviet-type economies.

   a. Compared to estimated U.S. annual growth rate of 4% between 1957-70, the U.S.S.R. will probably maintain an annual rate of 6.5%.

   b. Though the total gross national product (GNP) of the U.S.S.R. will be only 55% of that of the U.S. in 1970, present indications are that Soviet GNP will increase 130% during 1957-70, compared to 70% for the U.S. during the same period.

   c. By 1970, the U.S.S.R. may exceed U.S. in production capacity for non-consumer goods.

      (1) This is due to Soviet policy and capacity to allocate massive capital and labor to the industrial sector (heavy growth with little consumption).

2. Expanded industrialization will result in increased Soviet competition for free world and underdeveloped-area markets. (Centralized Soviet control over trade and technical assistance enhances capacity to influence world prices and future trade policies of underdeveloped areas.)

B. WESTERN EUROPE.

1. U.S. economic and military assistance aided Western Europe to attain unprecedented economic growth. (Combined gross national product is now within 10% of that of U.S. on basis of purchasing power equivalents.)

2. Estimated annual rate of Western European economic growth is 5.5%, not much less than that of Soviet Union.

3. Western Europe has now attained capacity to assist U.S. to increase trade and assistance to poorer areas.

C. OTHER AREAS. (Growth rates are harder to estimate because of lack of information.)

1. *China and India.*

   a. Their different economic systems account for Chinese growth of GNP at a ratio of 3 to 1 over India.

   b. Because of emphasis on production of consumer goods and encouragement of private sector, India needs substantial capital inflow from abroad.

2. *Latin America.*

    a. There are great variations in growth rate and potential of Latin American countries, but each depends on foreign markets for sale of basic commodities and on foreign sources for manufactured goods.

    b. Latin America has highest rate of population growth in world.

    c. Governments require capital from domestic savings, private investment, foreign governments, World and Inter-American Development Banks.

3. *Japan.*

    a. Future of Japan is not dependent on aid, but on ability to trade.

    b. If U.S. and European restrictionist policies become too severe, Japan may be forced to trade with Communist China.

II. ECONOMIC NEEDS OF UNDERDEVELOPED COUNTRIES.

A. INVARIABLE REQUIREMENT is for increase of capital intake from both internal and external sources, if "growth with consumption" is to be achieved.

    1. Unless underdeveloped countries acquire substantially larger amounts of investment capital than at present, by 1970 these countries will show less improvement in per capita income than developed countries. Without prospects of progress relative to the rest of the world, there is increased likelihood that Communist methods will be adopted.

    2. With 1% annual population growth, an investment of from 3 to 4% of national income yields static rates of per capita output, i.e., no growth at all.

        a. Population will grow from 1.5 to 2% per year in poorer countries.

        b. Consequently, in the poorer countries 5 to 8% of national income will have to be invested just to maintain present standards of living.

        c. Growth of per capita production and consumption in the 1960's will require a 100% increase of total capital inflow.

B. THE IMPORTANCE OF FREE TRADE.

    1. Growth rates of underdeveloped countries will depend on trade opportunities offered by industrial nations. Protectionist policies in U.S. and Western Europe inhibit growth in underdeveloped areas.

    2. Trade restrictions increase cost of raw materials, retarding expansion in industrial countries.

C. SOURCES OF CAPITAL FOR UNDERDEVELOPED AREAS.

1. Sources from industrialized countries of free world.
   a. In recent years, free world government loans and grants for economic aid and technical assistance have averaged $2 billion annually, of which over half has come from the U.S.
   b. International agencies have lent and granted over $800 million from 1954-57. This source is expanding.
   c. Non-U.S. loans and grants (mostly Western European) have tended to go to areas where the donor has political influence, e.g., the British Commonwealth or the French Community. The volume of loans and grants from this source could double or triple in the next decade.

2. Soviet economic aid.
   a. Soviet bloc extended credits and loans for about $2 billion from 1954-58. A little over $1 million was actually disbursed.
   b. Soviets generally concentrate aid on areas likely to have differences with West and often attach trade requirements to aid grants.

3. Private investment.
   a. U.S. government policy encourages private investment, but most goes to Canada and Western Europe. Oil and mineral-rich regions have received most of the remainder.
   b. Specific inducements for business to invest in underdeveloped areas are absolutely essential (e.g., Cooley amendment loans to private investors, and investment guarantee programs).

III. INTERNATIONAL TRADE—MAJOR FACTORS FOR FUTURE.

A. TOTAL WORLD TRADE DURING 1957-70 is likely to increase by about 50%, at the rate of 4% per year.

1. There will be great fluctuation in growth of trade in various areas.
   a. Imports of foodstuffs into industrial nations will probably increase by only 35%.
   b. Metal and ore imports will rise from 125 to 150%.
   c. Petroleum imports will increase even more than metals and ore.

2. Therefore, agricultural exporting countries will receive less capital from export of goods to foreign countries than exporters of minerals and petroleum. (To earn needed capital, foodstuff exporters must produce manufactured goods and develop new primary resources such as ore and petroleum.)

B. LIBERALIZATION OF TRADE RESTRICTIONS by Western Europe and U.S. would provide these developed countries with cheaper raw materials and enable poorer exporting countries to earn foreign exchange and become better customers.

C. U.S. MUST EXPAND ITS FOREIGN TRADE in order to promote its:

    1. International political influence.
    2. Internal economic growth.
    3. Long-run national security interests.

IV. U.S. BALANCE-OF-PAYMENTS DEFICIT — ITS RELATIONSHIP TO TRADE AND AID.

A. U.S. POSITION IN WORLD ECONOMY HAS CHANGED due to balance-of-payments deficit and loss of gold. *Deficit will not have an injurious effect on U.S. as long as U.S. maintains confidence in stability of the dollar and an internationally competitive position for its goods.*

    1. Foreign aid has contributed to balance-of-payments deficit by $13.5 billion over past 9 years. But it has added materially to the gold and dollar reserves of Western Europe and has satisfied U.S. aim of strengthening economic position of free world.

    2. Future U.S. economic policy depends in some measure on policies of foreign governments, e.g., whether a continued U.S. deficit will increase foreign dollar holdings or result in further gold loss.

B. BALANCE-OF-PAYMENTS DEFICIT LIKELY TO CONTINUE, given present commitments.

    1. U.S. imports likely to grow more rapidly than exports.

    2. Balance-of-payments will not be serious if U.S. promotes boost in exports.

        a. European Common Market restrictions can reduce some U.S. exports to that area and encourage establishment of U.S. European subsidiaries, which may increase deficit. However, these adverse effects on U.S. exports may be offset if the Common Market induces members' economic development.

        b. U.S. exports to underdeveloped countries will grow provided:
        (1) Developed countries invest in these countries and buy their products.
        (2) U.S. export prices compare favorably with those of other developed countries.

        c. Exports will also grow if U.S. exploits its great agricultural yield to become leading agricultural exporter.

    3. Overall increase in world trade will encourage foreign countries to increase their working balances of dollars and thus absorb some of the dollars generated by balance-of-payments deficit by not redeeming holdings for gold.

C. BALANCE-OF-PAYMENTS DEFICIT MUST NOT LEAD TO CURTAILMENT OF FOREIGN AID PROGRAM.

1. U.S. aid expenditures lead in large measure to growth in U.S. exports.
   a. 76% of all Mutual Security funds for commodities have been spent directly in U.S.
   b. Well planned economic aid can build up future markets for U.S. exports in aided countries and thus have little adverse effect on U.S. deficit.

2. The deficit leads to wider convertibility of currencies, increasing likelihood of repayment of our loans in dollars.

3. If, instead of demanding gold in payment of U.S. debts, Western Europe maintains large dollar balances, in effect, Western Europe is lending to U.S. U.S. position is then that of a "good banker" to underdeveloped countries, lending to them while borrowing from Western Europe.

4. Tying offers of U.S. assistance to purchases in U.S. should be considered only as last resort.

V. RECOMMENDATIONS.

A. DEVISE AN ECONOMIC STRATEGY to counter growing Communist economic and military threat. U.S. should lead allies in strategy which would exploit present superiority of free world over Communist in economic resources. Measures should be devised to:

1. Minimize normal conflicts of interest arising among industrial nations.

2. Mitigate conflicts of interest between industrial and underdeveloped nations.

3. Create a joint organization for the conduct of economic warfare, if Soviet tactics warrant it.

B. ORGANIZE A PROGRAM TO FOSTER DEVELOPMENT OF UNDERDEVELOPED AREAS.

1. U.S. should lead other industrial nations in fashioning common economic strategy focused on underdeveloped countries. This is as essential as a common military strategy.
   a. The common strategy would seek to define purposes, scope, and allocation of economic assistance.
      (1) Development loans should be made selectively, in amounts that can be absorbed productively, to countries of strategic importance with the best chance of developmental success.
      (2) Aid ought to be trebled or quadrupled by 1970.

    b. Steps should be undertaken to coordinate operations of various U.S. aid agencies and also to coordinate U.S. aid efforts with those of other governments and of regional and international agencies to produce more effective long-range economic development programs for underdeveloped countries.

  2. U.S. should revise its own aid program.

    a. Development Loan Fund (DLF) should be established on larger and more permanent basis with authorization to finance through public loans.

    b. Foreign currency deposits (counterpart funds) should be channeled into DLF or into International Development Association for development financing.

C. CREATE A U.S. POLICY FOR ECONOMIC GROWTH. Congress must examine U.S. growth prospects to determine policies most likely to produce expansion.

  1. Joint Economic Committee could undertake to examine our economic policies, aiming at removing legislative deterrents to growth which curb savings, restrict investment or encourage disinvestment, boost costs, limit trade and impose unnecessary rigidities on the economy.

  2. Congress and the Executive Branch should seek new policies designed to provide tax and other incentives for increased savings and investment by the public and corporations and thus provide resources necessary for growth.

  3. To forestall opposition of economically conservative groups, Congress should accompany the activities described above with objective statements of all issues involved in need for rapid growth.

  4. Similar examination is needed of those business and labor practices which inhibit growth by raising costs, restricting competition, reducing efficiency, limiting technological change, and imposing rigidities which hinder adjustments.

D. DEVELOP A COORDINATED APPROACH TO DOMESTIC AND FOREIGN POLICY ISSUES.

  1. Foreign Relations and Joint Economic Committees should consider joint study of those proposals which relate to domestic affairs but have foreign policy implications. Such joint studies would aim to minimize conflicts between domestic and foreign policy.

  2. Congress and Executive should resist growing demands for protection of domestic industries except where import competition threatens national defense.

E. EXPAND U.S. EXPORTS TO EASE BALANCE-OF-PAYMENTS PRESSURES.

  1. "An objective informational facility" should be established to make public facts relating to costs, prices, productive efficiency and other matters affecting the U.S. competitive position.
  2. This should encompass governmental policies such as surplus commodity pricing as well as labor-management negotiations on wages and other matters.

F. RE-EXAMINE U.S. SURPLUS DISPOSAL PROGRAM, which has tended to undercut normal markets of friendly nations.

  1. Senate Foreign Relations and Agriculture Committees should jointly consider program from the viewpoint of its impact on foreign relations.
  2. U.S. should consider establishing a surplus disposal program jointly with other surplus-producing areas to share benefits and losses.

Study No. 2

POSSIBLE NONMILITARY SCIENTIFIC DEVELOPMENTS AND THEIR POTENTIAL IMPACT ON FOREIGN POLICY PROBLEMS OF THE UNITED STATES

Stanford Research Institute
Menlo Park, California

Published: September 1959

41

GOALS OF THE REPORT

1. *To survey* the impact of past nonmilitary scientific developments on U.S. foreign policy.
2. *To identify* scientific developments likely to create foreign policy problems in the next decade.
3. *To forecast* some of the principal political, economic and social effects likely to result from these scientific developments so that foreign policy planners may prepare to cope with them.
4. *To indicate* areas in the nonmilitary applications of science where research and development could be positively used to benefit U.S. foreign policy.

MAJOR PREMISES OF THE REPORT

1. Scientific revolutions traditionally affect foreign policy. They tend, for example, to increase economic interdependence and destroy isolationism.
2. There is a time-lag between scientific developments and adjustment to them by individuals and societies.
3. Some scientific developments can be sufficiently well foreseen to enable preparation for them.
4. Accelerated scientific and technological developments will cause and intensify many foreign policy problems, thus calling for far greater planning.
5. Science and technology can provide tools for meeting many of the world's needs, and also provide areas for international cooperation.
6. Success in raising living standards and meeting basic demands in the underdeveloped and overpopulated areas will greatly influence our chances to maintain peace and stability in the world.
7. The broad directions of scientific development can to some extent be directed by governments and societies.
8. Much more research is needed in the sciences related to human behavior and social organization in order to be better able to deal with pressing human needs.

I. FORESEEABLE FOREIGN POLICY PROBLEMS CREATED BY SCIENTIFIC DEVELOPMENTS.

A. EFFECTS ON CONCEPTS OF NATIONAL SOVEREIGNTY.

    1. Worldwide scientific activities necessitate higher level of international cooperation and understanding. Examples of such activities are:

        a. Space vehicles. (An *ad hoc* committee of the U.N. has begun work on peaceful use of outer space, but the Communist bloc has not participated.)

        b. Radioactive fallout and nuclear wastes have created international tension over air and sea pollution—oceans, particularly, as they are a major source of food.

        c. Weather modification techniques (cloud seeding, fog dispersal) may lead to a means of climate control, with the danger of possible future "aggression" in this area.

        d. Mining of ocean floor for minerals and salts is technically possible, but additional study is needed on the location and extent of these resources.

    2. These activities present areas for international cooperation in which existing situations of national sovereignty need not be necessarily impaired.

B. EFFECTS ON PROGRAMS OF ECONOMIC AND SOCIAL DEVELOPMENT OF UNDERDEVELOPED AREAS.

    1. World hunger and population growth present major long-term international policy problems to the U.S. and other nations of the world.

        a. World population, according to U.N. estimates, will double in less than 50 years (to approximately 5 billion).

        (1) It is estimated that 30-50 years are needed to double agricultural productivity (to feed 4-5 billion people).

        (2) To increase food production to this extent would require a worldwide effort—approximately $10-15 billion a year in international aid.

        b. We can use science and technology to help increase food supplies through:

        (1) Sharing known methods.

        (a) Fertilizers, disease control, irrigation, use of reclaimed sewage.

        (b) Education in nutritional practices.

        (c) Improving our understanding of other peoples to assure their acceptance of our aid and advice.

        (2) Developing new methods of:

        (a) Inexpensive conversion of salt water.

        (b) More productive fishing techniques and pest control.

        (c) Producing new edible plants and synthetic proteins—work toward "breakthrough" in photosynthesis.

        (3) Developing a plan within the U.N. for surplus food disposal—U.S. should exert continued leadership (such as S. Res. 85 in 1955 for a world food bank).

  c. Population control is imperative in certain parts of world.

        (1) Japan, Puerto Rico, India, for example, have already taken steps to spread birth control methods.

        (2) New techniques of birth control are on the horizon and might be hastened by research programs carried on in cooperation with overpopulated countries. (At present only a few million dollars are annually spent on birth control, while $30 billion are spent on death control.)

2. Economic gap between more advanced countries and underdeveloped areas is widening, with 2/3 of world's population living in the latter. Lack of educational opportunities, etc., can cause even greater unrest than hunger.

  a. Results of past scientific developments in advanced countries and greatly improved world communications have induced among poorer peoples a "revolution of rising expectations."

        (1) Improved communications and Communist competition will produce even greater expectations and demands.

        (2) If these needs are not met by the free world, underdeveloped countries may turn to the Communists, with serious world political effects.

  b. Standards of living can be raised:

        (1) Immediately by greater diffusion of present knowledge.

        (2) In the future, through research in the physical and biological sciences and in the psychological and social sciences, e.g.:

           (a) Water desalination, solar energy, ocean resources, etc.

           (b) Administration, business management, techniques of diffusing knowledge, etc.

        (3) Through "adaptive invention" (adapting techniques of advanced nations to the specific needs of less developed areas).

  c. Research in psychological and social sciences is particularly needed to help the U.S. understand how to:

        (1) Best use developmental funds.

        (2) Select technical assistance personnel who can work with different cultures.

        (3) Best adapt programs to different areas (by understanding the role of government, private initiative, labor, etc., in countries with whom we are dealing).

C. EFFECTS ON WORLD TRADE PATTERNS.

1. World energy needs will have to be met mostly by conventional fuels (oil, gas, coal) for at least the next decade.

      a. Nuclear power will eventually be more important to countries now lacking energy resources, but not for at least a decade.

      b. Breakthrough in the science of solar energy could provide an important complementary source of energy for sunny areas where energy demands are not heavy.

2. U.S. will in the next decade become increasingly dependent on foreign resources for existing and new raw materials.

      a. U.S. must expect increased raw material and energy requirements in all countries including the underdeveloped areas.

      b. Adequate studies have yet to be published on this subject.

3. Displacement and obsolescence of commodities in world trade may become one of most difficult foreign policy problems.

      a. Introduction of synthetics (rubber, fibers, textiles, coffee, etc.) could drastically affect economies of (approximately 15) single-export countries.

      b. This could cause major economic setback in these areas, wipe out all benefits of U.S. aid, and cause major social unrest.

      c. Secondarily, it would reduce the amount of goods purchased in the U.S.

      d. Planning for these disruptions could help maintain stability in these areas.

4. U.S. business will confront increased competition and opportunities as areas industrialize.

      a. U.S. must analyze patterns of future world economic growth so that U.S. businesses can adapt to increased competition and opportunities.

      b. Trade restrictions will greatly reduce the chances of other countries developing in ways compatible with freedom.

      c. U.S. imports will enable countries selling to the U.S. to buy U.S. goods and repay U.S. loans and investments.

D. EFFECTS ON INTERNATIONAL COMMUNICATIONS.

1. U.S. policies need restudy and overhauling to meet problems arising from developments in both physical and psychological aspects of communication.

2. Development in physical means of communication:

      a. Technology will enable us to meet international telecommunications (radio, etc.) requirements, provided there is appropriate internal organization and the necessary international agreements.

      b. U.S. scientists must have access to foreign scientific works if they are to benefit from developments elsewhere. Communication of scientific knowledge by international information centers is now possible through machine translations.

      c. Diffusion of communications techniques throughout the world will increase, thus accelerating revolution of rising expectations.

      d. Study should be given to cheap news transmittal methods and to improved productive personal communications.

3. Developments in the psychological and social sciences might enable U.S. to better promote international progress.

   a. We must learn how to present new ideas and techniques to 'the underdeveloped areas, and to work within their cultures.

   b. Teacher shortages may possibly be eased by development and use of teaching machines.

   c. Developments in science of human behavior can create problems as well as help solve them.

      (1) They could provide means for totalitarian regimes to extend influence.

      (2) They could also offer possibilities for improved means of increasing international understanding, as in use of motivational research techniques to better understand forces motivating Americans and other peoples.

II. RECOMMENDATIONS.

A. DEVELOP A CONSCIOUS POLICY to promote foreign policy aims through a systematic stimulation of desirable nonmilitary scientific developments. Stimulate basic research and, when possible, foster international cooperation on research and scientific activity.

B. FOREIGN RELATIONS COMMITTEE should consider a three-part nonmilitary scientific program. It might request the Executive branch, in cooperation with the Committee staff and appropriate government agencies and/or private groups or individuals to:

   1. Prepare a list of specific foreign policy problems which would be aided by research and development, and propose ways of getting work stepped up or started. The following problems should be considered:

      a. Future scientific developments and their foreign policy impacts (e.g., development of synthetics).

      b. Scientific, political and legal aspects of activities conducted outside of national boundaries (e.g., in oceans, space, etc.).

      c. Food and population.

      d. Communications with other nations.

      e. International political organization, law and administration.

      f. New world trade relationships.

      g. Arms control and disarmament. (There should be a continuing study group with ample funds to subcontract to private groups.)

      h. Assistance in economic and social development of underdeveloped countries. (Charts pp. 90-92 of the study give specific examples of kinds of research needed.)

   2. Prepare a list of areas in which basic scientific research is required in order to aid U.S. foreign policy.

      a. Basic research is needed to develop theories about human behavior and interaction of economic, social and political events.

b. Motivational research is needed to evaluate such things as U.S. deterrence policy.

c. Some aspects of labor-management, industrial relations research can be applied to international relations.

3. Consider or propose new steps to encourage scientists' natural desire to cooperate with each other, in order to build bridges of understanding in the world, stimulating further scientific advancement.

a. Encourage scientific conferences and exchanges.

b. Promote international research programs, through the U.N. or in universities, possibly to be financed by funds from sales of surplus goods abroad (PL 480).

c. Encourage international exchange of scientific knowledge through machine translation system.

d. Lead in establishing an "International Development Year" to initiate studies on key development problems in underdeveloped areas, and stimulate basic research in sciences which might aid in their development.

e. Propose a U.N. university for advancement of science and humanities.

(1) To be on an advanced level, with branches throughout the world and having specialized institutes (e.g. World Institute of Social Technology).

(2) Might be financed by contributions of 1/10 of 1% of members' annual military defense expenditures or U.N. taxation of international resources newly opened by science (ocean resources, polar resources, space traffic rights).

Study No. 3

U.S. FOREIGN POLICY IN
WESTERN EUROPE

Foreign Policy Research Institute
University of Pennsylvania
Philadelphia, Pennsylvania

Published: October 15, 1959

GOALS OF THE REPORT

1. *To survey* the role of the 19-country Atlantic Community in the present world, with particular attention to the strategic importance of Western Europe.
2. *To analyze* the political, military and economic role of NATO countries in the defense and growth of the Western world, noting the:
   a. Interdependence of the United States and Western European countries.
   b. Development and strategic significance of supranational institutions in Europe.
3. *To postulate* a U.S. policy to strengthen the Western community, and thereby the entire free world.

MAJOR PREMISES OF THE REPORT

1. Western and Soviet ideologies and policies are unalterably and implacably opposed and competing.
2. The most salient single world problem is the intention of the Soviet Union to undermine Western power and ideology and to achieve world domination.
3. Europe is the primary objective of Soviet global strategy.
4. The future of the free world depends upon the strength and unity of the North Atlantic community of nations.
5. U.S.-European military alliance is logical and necessary as a defense against and preventive to Soviet aggression.
6. Far closer political and economic alliance should be developed among the North Atlantic nations (including U.S.). Such alliance:
   a. Is facilitated by common cultural and spiritual heritage.
   b. Requires common defense policy.
   c. Requires within it supranational institutions:
      (1) To promote closely linked economic plans to facilitate steady growth in and constructive relations with underdeveloped nations.
      (2) To cope with consequences of technological development and political revolution.
7. It is out-dated to depend too rigidly on the nation-state alone to guarantee the welfare or security of its people.
8. Western traditions share the basic goal of promotion of freedom for all men; if the strength of Western civilization is to be maintained, these traditions must be universalized.
9. Closest collaboration among all Atlantic countries, colonial and non-colonial, is essential to assure gradual and peaceful integration of the emergent nations into the free world.

I. POLITICAL FACTORS AFFECTING EUROPEAN UNITY.

A. PRESENT EUROPEAN COOPERATION IS PRINCIPALLY MILITARY AND ECONOMIC.

1. European attitudes toward political unity have varied with the ebb and flow of Soviet threats.
2. Private and governmental groups working to devise forms of European, Atlantic or regional political unity have lacked mass support, leadership, and clearly defined programs.
3. Potential "exclusiveness" of certain supranational arrangements (e.g., the Common Market) could promote economic discrimination and, therefore, disunity.

B. ROLE OF POLITICAL PARTIES IN UNIFICATION.

1. *Christian Democratic parties* have favored European integration but are losing popular support and lack young leaders.
2. *Socialists* increasingly support nationalism and neutralism, though have favored some integration.
3. *Communists* often use other parties through "popular Fronts," stressing nationalism and garnering middle-class vote by disguising Soviet orientation. (Party is strongest in France and Italy.)

C. ROLE OF NATIONALISM.

1. Nationalism in the Atlantic Community aims to acquire for a nation equal voice in the alliance; it has not tended to undermine European cooperation.
   a. The preferred position given Britain by the U.S. has resulted in resentment on the continent of Anglo-American alignment.
   b. U.S. failure to consult with all allies and to assure equality may promote competing groups of states, undermining Atlantic Community concept.
2. Technological advance and desire for economic betterment have led to push for economic, but not political, coordination.

D. ROLE OF NEUTRALISM IN THE ATLANTIC COMMUNITY.

1. Neutralism is characterized by:
   a. Suspicion of U.S. policy.
   b. Cultural anti-Americanism.
   c. Fear of war.
   d. Defeatism due to belief of inevitability of Soviet advance.
2. It is frequently expressed in adherence to "third force" concept, uniting Europe as an independent force and arbiter between U.S. and Communist bloc.
3. It tends to involve basic hostility to the idea of NATO as a European-U.S. alliance.

II. MILITARY FACTORS AFFECTING EUROPEAN SECURITY.

A. PURPOSE OF NATO to:
1. Provide complete military defense of Western Europe.
2. Provide military backing adequate for the effective conduct of Western diplomacy.
3. Prevent Soviets from launching total or limited nuclear or conventional aggression for fear of too costly retaliation. (Extremely unlikely that NATO powers would initiate conflict.)

B. PRESENT NATIONAL DEFENSES NEITHER ADEQUATE NOR SUFFICIENTLY FLEXIBLE.
1. Western capacity for "deterrence" (maintaining forces sufficient to make possible cost of attack too great) increasingly weak as Soviet nuclear capacity grows.
    a. Current weapons systems and strategy do not adequately provide for all the contingencies of total, limited, nuclear or ground war.
    b. Nuclear war would be difficult to limit in Europe due to heavy population density and proximity of military to civilian targets.
    c. NATO defenses are weak in conventional forces (army, navy, air) and inadequate to needs of local defense.
2. Nuclear weapons necessary for balanced NATO defense are not yet integrated into overall strategy.
    a. Soviet forces have them.
    b. "Balance" does not mean matching the Soviets item for item, but being prepared to meet any kind of offensive with forces that will prevent protracted aggression and all-out holocaust.
    c. Nuclear forces for NATO would provide greater flexibility of defense and indicate greater trust in European allies.

C. SOVIET THREATS BACKED BY SUPERIOR MILITARY STRENGTH TEND TO DEMORALIZE AND DIVIDE NATO.
1. Growing Soviet nuclear capacity increases power to achieve objectives even without aggression.
2. Western counter strategy requires immediate decisions on policies to be carried out five years from now.

D. DISENGAGEMENT PROPOSALS IMPRACTICAL. Disengagement would:
1. Create vacant area which invites aggression.
2. Assume stable "balance of terror." However, technological changes make balance inherently unstable.
3. Require dissolution of the foundation of Western strategy and defense, i.e., NATO and the Atlantic alliance.

E. LIMITED GRADUAL DISARMAMENT POSSIBLE.

1. This is a feasible alternative to disengagement.
2. Efforts to achieve decrease of arms have failed to date, because:
   a. Soviets refuse adequate inspection system.
   b. West's military strategy, by overstressing nuclear and understressing conventional weapons, has made for disproportionate balance between Soviet Union and West.

III. RELEVANCE OF ECONOMIC COOPERATION.

A. IMPORTANCE OF WESTERN EUROPEAN ECONOMIC STRENGTH TO FREE WORLD.

1. Western Europe is a decisive economic support in the struggle against Communist bloc.
2. Rate of European economic expansion exceeded that of both the U.S. and U.S.S.R. in last decade.

B. COOPERATIVE ECONOMIC ORGANIZATIONS INCREASE EUROPEAN ECONOMIC STRENGTH.

1. Expanded markets resulting from Coal and Steel Community, Common Market, Euratom, etc., have decreased costs.
2. Formation of rival economic groups, however, is potentially destructive to both political and economic strength of North Atlantic nations (competition, for example, between "Inner Six" of Common Market and the British-led "Outer Seven").

C. WESTERN ECONOMIC RELATIONS WITH UNDERDEVELOPED AREAS.

1. Western nations need continued friendship of underdeveloped areas, as:
   a. Sources of raw materials.
   b. Potential markets.
   c. Force for independence and opposition to Communism.
2. Trade ties are likely to contribute more effectively than strengthened aid programs to stable, planned economic growth of underdeveloped nations.
3. Present development programs are uncoordinated, haphazard.
4. Government programs are necessary initially but as encouragement to growth of private capital investment.

D. EAST-WEST TRADE.

1. Industrial development of Europe, Asia and Africa will invite increased Soviet trade offers and add to lure of Soviet markets.

2. Policy of exchanging Western manufacturing equipment for Soviet consumer goods is extremely dangerous.
   a. Strengthened Soviet productive capacity increases Soviet ability to achieve world domination.
   b. Lack of sufficient export opportunities has led Britain, France and West Germany to increase trade with the Soviet Union.

IV. RECOMMENDATIONS FOR U.S. POLICY IN WESTERN EUROPE.

A. STRENGTHENING THE NATO MILITARY ALLIANCE AND UNIFYING THE ATLANTIC COMMUNITY in both political and economic fields should be an overriding U.S. foreign policy objective during the next decade.

B. U.S. SHOULD ENCOURAGE MOVES TO STRENGTHEN EUROPEAN MILITARY UNITY.

1. Assist NATO to develop sufficient retaliatory power to deter Soviets from nuclear as well as conventional ground aggression.
   a. Equip NATO with strategic nuclear force for European defense. Develop "clean" nuclear weapons, but do not permit them to be indispensable for every military encounter.
   b. Build NATO's tactical nuclear and conventional strength to point where Western Europe can be defended with or without nuclear weapons.
      (1) Increase NATO force to 30 ready divisions and create 60 reserve divisions, maintaining 1/3 of reserves ready for one-week mobilization.
      (2) Build mobile reserve capacity (submarines, missile and air units) for nuclear and nonnuclear combat.
      (3) Increase Strategic Air Command forces which are capable of rapid deployment in Western Europe and elsewhere.
2. Share U.S. nuclear knowledge with principal European allies to avoid:
   a. Duplication of development effort.
   b. Diversion by them of funds for buildup of ground forces.
3. Begin joint research, construction and financing of armaments, to allow for:
   a. More specialization.
   b. Decreased costs.
   c. More rapid and less overlapping development.

C. U.S. SHOULD ENCOURAGE MOVES TOWARD EUROPEAN POLITICAL UNITY.

1. Support existing unifying organizations (Euratom, Coal and Steel Community, Common Market).

a. Discourage any attempts at exclusion or discrimination by Common Market group.

b. Attempt to reconcile divisive interests of NATO partners; avoid favoring any one nation.

2. Encourage consultation among North Atlantic states.

   a. Assure Western European nations of American intention to consult with them prior to announcement of major policy commitments. Building economic and military strength is more important than complete compliance with American policy.

   b. Support proposal of June 1959 Atlantic Congress for conference of leading citizens to explore channels of further cooperation.

   c. Take lead in establishing regular consultation among government representatives and heads of government and set up tribunal for friendly settlement of disputes among nations in this area.

3. Support progressive policies toward dependent areas.

   a. Urge moves toward self-government and independence for qualified dependent peoples.

   b. Support development of British Commonwealth of Nations and French Community.

D. U.S. SHOULD ENCOURAGE MOVES TOWARD EUROPEAN ECONOMIC UNITY.

1. Encourage and cooperate with Common Market countries in creating freer world markets, subject to two conditions:

   a. That tariffs erected around Common Market nations not be raised.

   b. That rival economic arrangements (such as European Free Trade Association and Common Market) do not adversely affect further economic growth or political solidarity of Western Europe.

2. Support creation of new Office for Atlantic Economic Cooperation, as proposed at 1959 Atlantic Congress, in order to:

   a. Provide greater degree of economic cooperation and regulation than does the General Agreement on Tariffs and Trade (GATT).

   b. Meet Soviet trade challenge and prevent development of Europe into "third force" between East and West.

3. Stress danger of trade with Soviets of all industrial goods—not only those with potential military use.

4. Persuade allies, in their trade policies with Communist bloc countries, to agree to:

   a. Sell only in exchange for convertible currencies.

   b. Refrain from extending any credit.

   c. Minimize sale of capital goods and concentrate on consumer goods sales.

       d. Prevent Communist bloc penetration of European markets (through dumping or similar devices).

       e. Free economically weaker Western states (e.g., Iceland) from dependence on Soviet trade.

   5. Plan with European allies ways in which they may begin to contribute larger share of NATO budget and economic assistance, and develop combined government-private enterprise approach to aiding underdeveloped countries.

   6. Encourage fullest possible industrial development of the atom to meet Europe's future energy needs, and insure that international agreements banning nuclear tests allow for such usage.

   7. Encourage long-term joint planning toward underdeveloped areas by metropolitan nations, to:

       a. Invest as much as these areas can absorb.

       b. Create new mechanisms which will:

          (1) Link Western industrial expansion with an effort to stabilize prices of primary products in underdeveloped countries.

          (2) Foster the growth of nongovernmental enterprise.

   8. Plan for increased economic coordination in order to:

       a. Increase productivity and lower costs.

       b. Contribute to political unity.

       c. Counter Soviet economic challenge.

E. (Additional policy recommendations to be found in section V under A-2, B-2, and C-2.)

V. APPENDICES.

(This report contains at the end six appendices and a glossary of terms. The appendices approximate policy papers on discrete European problems. Because they were not integrated into the text, they are outlined separately here.)

A. WESTERN EUROPE AND THE NON-ATLANTIC WORLD.

   1. Background.

       a. Politically and economically, Europe's future well-being necessitates ties with non-Atlantic world.

          (1) Economically necessary for outside markets and raw materials.

          (2) Politically necessary as support in cold war and base for defense.

       b. Underdeveloped countries are vitally concerned to attain political and economic independence.

          (1) Unified in their desire for economic progress and for equality in international community (thus very anti-colonial).

          (2) Often skeptical of West's motives, due to:

             (a) Colonial history of European powers.

             (b) Lack of clarity and unity in Western nations' policy statements of their intentions and goals.

    c. Primary objective of international communism is to undermine European position, through clearcut political support of moves toward independence. Thereby, Communists are establishing a mutuality of Communist and anti-colonial interests.

2. Recommendations:

    a. Western policies must emphasize mutual interests of Atlantic and non-Atlantic world, indicating:

        (1) Atlantic states' need for sources of supply, markets, bases.

        (2) Need by non-Atlantic states for trade, capital investment, technical assistance.

        (3) Unanimity in both worlds on the basic objectives of all free peoples.

    b. Long-term planning by all metropolitan powers in consultation with each other is essential:

        (1) To achieve peaceful transition of African territories to independent states.

        (2) To convince non-Atlantic nations of West's united concern for genuine independence and economic advance.

    c. Increased European economic unity will benefit both Atlantic and non-Atlantic communities, enhancing:

        (1) Greater productivity, through:

            (a) Increased demand for raw materials at more stable price levels.

            (b) Decreased manufacturing costs and cheaper goods.

        (2) More coordinated, less competitive long-range planning regarding the non-Atlantic areas.

B. EASTERN EUROPE'S MEANING TO THE WEST.

1. Background.

    a. Russia's European satellites are perhaps the most anti-Communist, anti-Russian forces in the world today.

        (1) Satellites are resentful of economic exploitation, political subservience, loss of national identity.

        (2) Soviets are most vulnerable in satellites.

    b. East-West division of Europe is unnatural culturally and economically.

    c. U.S. has failed to take initiative in policies which would support and encourage the freedom of Eastern European nations.

2. Recommendations.

    a. West must support unequivocally and actively, with every possible peaceful means, the right of the peoples of Eastern Europe to self-determination and freedom.

        (1) Expand cultural exchanges.

        (2) Encourage trade and commerce with the West.

        (3) Support humanitarian drives (as by former shipment of food to Poland).

C. EUROPE'S ENERGY PROBLEM.

1. Background.
   a. Continuing growth of European economy puts strain on conventional sources of power (coal, oil, hydroelectric).
   b. Oil supply sources are increasingly diversified (Arab countries, South America, Algeria, Soviet Union) and include possible new methods of extraction from shale.
   c. Further exploration of nuclear power utilization is likely.
2. Recommendation.
   a. Advantageous economic understandings between European and Arab countries should be encouraged to prevent Soviet oil dumping.

D. THE UNITED STATES AND SPAIN.

1. Spain's strategic geographical position accounts for close U.S. military ties.
2. It is unlikely that Spain will be admitted to NATO in near future despite U.S. policy of encouraging closer ties.
3. Its economy is not yet strong enough to join Common Market or Outer Seven.
4. Continued dependence mainly on U.S. for international support and recognition is probable.

E. STATISTICAL ANALYSES. Three graphs and charts as follows:

1. Gross national product from 1948 to 1957 of member countries in Organization for European Economic Cooperation (OEEC).
2. Volume of basic commodities produced in 1957 by members of OEEC and other countries.
3. Comparative trade patterns in 1948 and 1957 of OEEC countries, the U.S., Sino-Soviet bloc and other world areas.

Study No. 4

U.S. FOREIGN POLICY IN AFRICA

Program of African Studies
Northwestern University
Evanston, Illinois

Published: October 23, 1959

GOALS OF THE REPORT

1. *To survey* the countries south of the Sahara with regard to:
   a. Main internal trends and problems.
   b. Background of U.S.-Africa relations.
   c. Main U.S. foreign policy problems with regard to Africa.
   d. U.S.-Africa relations in the U.N.
2. *To recommend* policies and programs to enhance relations between the U.S. and Africa.

MAJOR PREMISES OF THE REPORT

1. Africa has a new significance in world politics with implications for U.S. domestic as well as foreign policy. It is important that the U.S. appreciate these implications.
2. The U.S. has a responsibility to pursue a much more vigorous policy toward Africa. Meeting this responsibility involves:
   a. Faithfulness to our own expressed values, e.g., racial tolerance, self-determination.
   b. Helpful response to the pressing economic, social, educational and other needs of developing African nations.
3. The basic pro-Western orientation of Africa is strong and Africa will tend to look to the U.S. for support of its political positions and assistance in its economic and social development. African states will nonetheless insist on pursuing development goals without getting involved in the East-West power struggle.
4. The U.S. can work with the new African states whether or not they develop democratic institutions which follow Western models.

I. MAIN AFRICAN TRENDS AND INTERNAL PROBLEMS.

A. POLITICAL.

1. Rapid proliferation of new, independent states.
   a. By the end of 1959, six countries were independent: Ethiopia, Liberia, Union of South Africa, Sudan, Ghana and Guinea.
   b. By the end of 1960, independent states will also include: Nigeria, Togo, Somalia, French Cameroons and the Federation of Mali. Possibly also the British Cameroons.*
   c. By 1970, 20 or 25 sub-Saharan countries will be independent.

---

* Since issuance of this report, the following have received independence: Belgian Congo and the French-speaking nations of Ivory Coast, Dahomey, Niger, Upper Volta, Gabon, Republic of the Congo, Chad, Central African Republic, and Malagasy. The Federation of Mali has since broken up into Senegal and Mali.

   2. Other salient political features:

      a. The stages of transition from colonial control to autonomy (self-determination in internal affairs)—to independence—have been generally peaceful.

      b. The emergent political regimes are based on various combinations of tribal and colonial heritages with the results ranging from traditional absolutist monarchy—to constitutional oligarchy —to parliamentary democracy.

      c. One-party systems based on wide popular support, accompanied by strong executives and weak legislatures, are likely to be prevailing patterns of power in the future. Political maneuvering will tend to be within a party framework.

   3. Major internal political problem areas.

      a. A major, unresolved problem is the method and speed by which those countries having a substantial non-African population will share political power with the African majority.

      b. Persistent anti-colonial feelings plus a firm determination to remain independent of the East-West power struggle are likely to lead to:

        (1) Growth of pan-African organizations,

        (2) Joint or similar foreign policies, and

        (3) Federations of states (with possible revisions of arbitrary boundaries set by colonial powers).

      c. Independence has thus far been achieved through constitutional change and there is a general commitment to constitutionalism. Nonetheless, the shaping of constitutions will be a persistent problem, particularly as constitutions govern the relationships and responsibilities of citizens to the colonial power.

      d. There is little indigenous communism and, except in a few areas, little evidence of substantial Communist penetration.

B. ECONOMIC.

   1. 75% of Africans are engaged in subsistence agriculture.

   2. Trade with and investment by colonial powers has been the principal source of development to date.

   3. Natural resource potential is great, but unevenly distributed (e.g., vast hydroelectric potential and scattered but large oil and mineral deposits).

   4. Major internal economic problem areas.

      a. Effective utilization of their natural resources requires:

        (1) Increased technical assistance.

        (2) Acquisition of foreign capital as well as accumulation of capital through local savings and taxation.

        (3) Stimulation of internal and external trade with departure from one-export economies; diversification of foreign customers

with increased variety in crop, mineral and industrial development.

(4) Education leading to acceptance of modern land-improvement methods, e.g., irrigation, crop rotation, fertilization.

C. SOCIAL.

1. Tradition.
   a. Emerging political and economic institutions will be influenced by traditional social concepts (e.g., patterns of authority, prestige and responsibility).
   b. While not necessarily undemocratic and often well organized, these patterns can increasingly conflict with those of "modern" leaders.
2. Race.
   a. There are three major racial groupings: Black Africans, Indians and Africans of European background. Only 3% of sub-Saharan Africa is non-native African.
   b. Major sources of friction exist where economic privilege and political power are related to color—where white privilege has been institutionalized.
3. Education.
   a. There is great pressure throughout Africa to increase educational opportunity. A high proportion of African budgets are now devoted to education.
   b. Illiteracy is approximately 80%.
   c. While percentage gains are impressive, emphasis on education began only after World War II; therefore, shortage of trained personnel is acute.
4. Language.
   a. With over 800 separate languages in sub-Saharan Africa, nationalism along linguistic lines unlikely to develop.
5. Labor.
   a. Union membership now small, but growing along with growth of cities. As in Ghana, likely to develop in environment of strong government control.

II. BACKGROUND OF U.S.-AFRICA RELATIONS.

A. U.S. GOVERNMENT ACTIVITY.

1. Past.
   a. With exception of Liberia, prior to 1956 U.S. showed only minor interest in African affairs.
   b. U.S. revolutionary, anti-colonial past has served as symbol to African nations seeking self-government. While this has stood U.S. in good stead, America is being increasingly lumped in with the image of Western colonial powers.

2. Present.
   a. *Military*. Present U.S. commitments to sub-Saharan Africa are minimal.
   b. *Economic*. U.S. grants and loans are proportionately small. As independent countries proliferate, there is increased demand, particularly for personnel and equipment to assist in development.
   c. *Educational*. African states urgently desire and welcome international assistance for secondary and higher education, teacher training, technical, vocational and professional education, as well as increased opportunities for training overseas.

B. U.S. PRIVATE ACTIVITY.

1. Economic.
   a. Private investment is relatively small, and confined mainly to Liberia and Union of South Africa.
   b. Increase is dependent on further assurances of high investment return, political stability and encouragement by African governments.
2. Missionary.
   a. Past influence has been strong in religion, education, health and agriculture but declines as local contacts with other foreigners broaden.

III. CHIEF U.S. FOREIGN POLICY PROBLEMS REGARDING AFRICA.

A. PROBLEM OF BALANCING U.S. OBLIGATIONS TO NATO COUNTRIES (colonial powers) and African states. U.S. is pulled in opposing directions by urgent African demands for self-government and anti-colonial sentiment on the one hand, and recalcitrance and gradualism of European powers (especially of European African settlers) on the other.

1. The growth of U.S. economic and cultural participation with African countries will frequently be impeded by persisting economic and cultural ties with former colonial powers.
2. The U.N. African Caucusing Group expects a clearly liberal stand by the U.S. on such cases as the pending drive on behalf of the strictly-controlled Portuguese colonial territories.
3. U.S. must prepare to deal with following dilemmas resulting from the sense of common cause existing between sub-Saharan and North African countries:
   a. General sub-Saharan support for Algerian independence.
   b. Feeling that European Common Market interests in Africa may inhibit expanded African trade. U.S. encouragement of (or participation in) increased trade with African countries may tend to promote policy conflicts with Europe.

c. Unanimous African opposition to French atomic explosions in the Sahara.

B. PROBLEMS OF U.S. POSTURE TOWARD AFRICAN RACIAL DIFFICULTIES.

1. U.S. can anticipate increasing pressure to declare support for or against African self-government in face of entrenched white settler-dominated government. Posture of detachment virtually impossible because of:

   a. Prominence of the race problem inside the U.S.
   b. Record of U.S. support for independence already established in some areas.

2. U.S. policy-makers must be wary of danger in confusing African pro-nationalism with anti-white sentiment. By and large, Africans welcome European (i.e., white) participation, but resent white privilege.

C. PROBLEMS OF ECONOMIC RELATIONS.

1. With dependent territories.

   a. U.S. investment and capital assistance should include opportunities for African participation, advancement and responsibility.
   b. Dilemmas arise when local businesses and governments oppose such increased opportunities for Africans.

2. With independent states.

   a. Most African countries, lacking sufficient internal capital for economic growth, will thus depend on foreign aid and investment for initial expansion.
   b. The selection of countries, types of projects, amount and methods of allocating assistance to more than 20 African nations will pose large continuing problems of evaluation and choice for the U.S.
      (1) Support of regional projects, though to be encouraged, should not be imposed.
      (2) Conventional plans for economic development will require modification in light of local political, social or religious factors.

3. With African states involved in agreement with non- or anti-U.S. sources of assistance.

   a. Aid will be requested of international bodies such as World Bank, of former colonial powers, of other European nations, of the U.S., and of Sino-Soviet bloc.
   b. U.S. must learn to adjust to the indiscriminate petitioner at risk of isolating itself from particular area.

D. **PROBLEMS OF DEMOCRACY IN SUB-SAHARAN AFRICA.**

    1. U.S. faces long-term dilemma on question of supporting African nations which will, in all likelihood, be only partially democratic.

    2. Judicious use of aid can assist in building the cultural and economic bases which are prerequisites of democratic institutions.

E. **PROBLEMS OF NON-ALIGNMENT AND AFRICAN POSITIONS OF NEUTRALITY.**

    1. Non-alignment in East-West struggle is likely throughout Africa. Generally, Africans covet independence once it is obtained.

    2. Though underlying pro-Western orientation is evident in African desire for democracy and in their institutions and customs, most Africans want foreign contacts and assistance on as wide a basis as possible. They view East-West power struggle as an external problem.

IV. U.S.-AFRICAN RELATIONS IN THE U.N.

A. **ANALYSIS OF U.S. VOTING RECORD ON AFRICAN MATTERS IN THE U.N.** discloses:

    1. U.S. has been substantially more in agreement with anti-colonial powers than with NATO associates.

    2. To African nations, U.S. posture has appeared ambiguous and needs clarification: U.S. abstention on Algerian independence vote viewed by Africans as pro-colonial, while recent U.S. vote "against" South Africa on U.N. jurisdiction in South-West Africa was widely praised.

B. **DEVELOPMENT OF AFRICAN CAUCUSING GROUP.**

    1. African Caucusing Group maintains increasing position of influence in U.N. Entry of six additional states in 1960 is evidence of increasing power.

    2. During two years' existence, group voted together 46.7% of time on all issues.

V. POLICY RECOMMENDATIONS.

A. **U.S. MUST UNDERTAKE LONG-RANGE PLANNING** and goal formulation toward Africa.

B. **U.S. MUST TREAT AFRICA AS A MAJOR POLICY AREA** equivalent to Europe. U.S. must:

    1. *Take stand in favor of self-government of African states.* Extend to all states policy applied to Tanganyika, favoring advance timetables for moves toward independence in the interest of peaceful transition.

2. *Respect African policies of non-alignment.* Place political considerations and technical assistance ahead of military aid and strategic requirements.

3. *Proceed with flexible policies.* Maintain awareness that the cultural heritage affecting the rising leadership is vastly different from that of Western countries.

4. *Clarify stand on racial segregation.* Apply non-discriminatory hiring policies to embassy and consular staffs as well as to other types of U.S. enterprise in Africa.

C. U.S. SHOULD EXTEND FINANCIAL ASSISTANCE to variety of African needs. It should:

1. Provide substantial assistance to education.
   a. Support secondary, higher, technical, professional, teacher training and exchange of persons programs, through:
      (1) Scholarship and special training programs in the U.S.
      (2) Financial assistance to African nations.
   b. Encourage establishment of multi-national educational advisory bodies which can adjust and adapt American standards and techniques to the needs of African countries.

2. Provide technical assistance with primary aim of training Africans to carry forth programs in their own countries.

3. Assist moves to establish career services for technical assistance personnel on the international level.

4. Encourage development of regional groupings (e.g., Colombo Plan) to facilitate multi-national programming of foreign aid.

5. Emphasize aid toward basic development projects which presently receive too little support due to inadequate local capital and personnel.

6. Encourage U.S. aid agencies to utilize growing numbers of African specialists in non-governmental institutions and to undertake studies on best means for U.S. to stimulate long-term economic growth and stability in Africa.

7. Assist American private capital investment in Africa.
   a. Extend Department of Commerce African economic study series to include information on industrial and commercial development potential in additional countries.
   b. Extend International Cooperation Administration investment guarantee program to independent African states.

Study No. 5

U.S. FOREIGN POLICY IN ASIA

Conlon Associates, Ltd.
310 Clay Street
San Francisco, California

Published: November 1, 1959

GOALS OF THE REPORT

1. *To project and analyze* major trends in Asia over the next decade. (In the interest of brevity, this outline does not include the report's analysis of *trends* in Asia.)
2. *To make recommendations* for U.S. policy in Asia.

MAJOR PREMISES OF THE REPORT

1. U.S. ability to influence basic forces at work in Asia is *limited* and depends on use of existing assets.
   a. U.S. assets in Asia include: our material wealth, technological and administrative skills, military strength, experience with democratic institutions, and reservoir of good will.
   b. By wise use of these assets in Asia, U.S. can (somewhat) influence the: .
   (1) Course and speed of economic growth.
   (2) Nature of social change.
   (3) Degree of security from foreign aggression.
   (4) Asian appreciation of democratic institutions.
   c. The countries of Asia will increase their ties with the rest of the world as extreme nationalism is modified by growing economic strength and political maturity. However, as the influence of India, China, and Japan grows and as Asia develops its own system of power politics, the relative influence of the U.S. and U.S.S.R. will decrease.
2. The ability of Asian countries to withstand Communism in the long run depends on their political, economic and social—rather than military—strength.

I. RECOMMENDED U.S. POLICIES TOWARD ASIA (AS A WHOLE).

A. ECONOMIC. U.S. must:

1. Assist in formulating and executing realistic, long-range national development programs providing for:
   a. Balanced economic and social progress at a rate rapid enough to satisfy rising individual expectations.
   b. Maintenance of all possible individual freedoms while keeping political tensions to a minimum.
2. Assist Asian leaders in identifying and directly attacking social problems.
3. Continue substantial, and probably increase, U.S. economic aid and technical assistance.
4. Foster multilateral cooperation in aid programs.
   a. Explore possibilities of joint aid programs with other nations, including the U.S.S.R.
   b. Maintain support of U.N. assistance programs.

5. Promote regional cooperation among Asian countries by:

   a. Creating a regional development bank, financed by U.S., Western Europe, and Japan and administered by Asians.

   b. Creating regional technical centers and regional payment plans.

   c. Expanding the Economic Commission for Asia and the Far East (ECAFE) and the Colombo plan while refraining from expanding South East Asia Treaty Organization (SEATO) into non-military areas.

   d. Developing more programs like the Indus and Mekong River projects and the southeast Asia telecommunications project.

6. Promote foreign trade and foreign investment in Asia as a means of fostering economic development.

   a. If U.S. and Europe are to expand their exports of capital and technical skills, they must find ways to absorb more Asian imports.

   b. An effort must be made to stabilize prices of commodities on which limited-crop economies depend.

   c. U.S. must utilize its surplus commodities to alleviate food shortages (without disrupting commodity prices).

B. POLITICAL. In formulating and executing U.S. policy, U.S. must:

1. Take Asian attitudes more effectively into account by:

   a. More policy consultation with Asians.

   b. Further use of joint agencies to administer aid, information and cultural exchange programs.

2. Develop continuing contact with all major political and social factions in a country ("diplomacy in depth"), by:

   a. Increasing contacts of U.S. officials with Asian leaders.

   b. Encouraging contacts of non-official Americans (e.g., businessmen, educators) with Asians.

3. Cooperate more effectively with governments which are not antagonistic to U.S., but which may frequently differ with us on specific policies. U.S., for example, must understand:

   a. Neutrality regarded by Asians as a means to maintain newly-won independence and concentrate on internal problems.

   b. Strong nationalism of Asians and their sensitivity to threat of foreign influence, whether by U.S. or Communist nations.

4. Develop real cultural interaction between U.S. and Asia by:

   a. Strengthening image of U.S. by emphasizing not only our material prosperity but also our dynamism, creativity, and desire for peace.

   b. Promoting cultural exchange programs, trade fairs, U.S. cultural centers.

C. MILITARY: U.S. should appoint an American civilian-military team to re-examine U.S. military strategy in Asia in light of:
1. Total U.S. strategic objectives in Asia.
2. U.S. political and economic objectives in Asia.

II. RECOMMENDED U.S. POLICIES TOWARD SOUTH ASIA.

A. GENERAL. U.S. should:
1. Foster regional economic cooperation so that the various South Asian countries coordinate their economic planning instead of engaging in wasteful competition.
2. Encourage solutions to problems causing discord in the area, e.g., the Kashmir dispute. This will enable these countries, particularly India and Pakistan, to concentrate more of their resources on economic development.

B. INDIA: U.S. should:
1. Encourage contact by U.S. personnel with all political parties of democratic persuasion, not just the Congress Party.
2. If one should arise, encourage a national government in which all responsible democratic parties would cooperate to deal·with India's vast economic and social problems. Such a government is advocated by Mehta of the Praja Socialist Party.
3. Recognize need for more authority by Indian central government to ensure social and economic development and political stability.
4. Assist India to reach point of self-sustained economic growth· by:
   a. Considering negotiation of an aid agreement between India, U.S., U.S.S.R., perhaps Japan, Western Germany or others.
      (1) Agreement would make possible long-range (10-year) commitments to support given sectors of India's third and fourth five-year plans.
      (2) Donor nations would be invited by India to advise on detailed planning process.
   b. Providing the bulk of the $1 billion foreign aid needed annually by India. To do this, Congress should either:
      (1) Pass special legislation tailored to India's needs (or those of whatever given South Asian country). Legislation should be based on plans covering the next decade which could be evolved at a meeting between a joint Congressional-Executive delegation and representatives of the government concerned, *or*
      (2) Grant more long-term DLF funds with amounts earmarked for India.
   c. Allocating increased DLF and PL 480 funds to private sector of Indian economy.

    d. Giving India—in additon to increased aid—constructive criticism on her development efforts. U.S. will, however, have to:

      (1) Rely on basic planning by Indians themselves.

      (2) Recognize India's goal of a soeialist mixed economy.

C. NEPAL. U.S. should:

1. Continue modest aid program of economic and technical assistance.
2. Increase informational, educational, cultural activity.
3. Consult informally with Nepalese and Indian governments on programs for Nepal.

D. CEYLON. U.S. should:

1. Recognize that conditions will not be favorable to substantial economic development in Ceylon for some time.
2. Increase U.S. aid cautiously on the basis of Ceylon's new economic plans and after consultation between U.S. and Ceylonese officials.
3. Endeavor to achieve international regularization of rubber purchases—even at subsidy rates—to help alleviate Ceylon's economic woes, which otherwise might get worse.

E. PAKISTAN. U.S. should:

1. Make special efforts to encourage Pakistan's full economic development, so India will not to a marked degree continue to outstrip Pakistan.

    a. U.S. technical assistance, as well as U.S. economic aid, should be increased substantially.

    b. U.S. should urge Pakistan to cut down on budgetary priority given her military establishment.

2. Try at appropriate time to effect mutual defense and partial disarmament agreement between India and Pakistan to release energies for more constructive purposes.

III. RECOMMENDED U.S. POLICIES TOWARD SOUTHEAST ASIA.

A. POLITICAL. U.S. should:

1. Recognize that conditions for democracy do not yet exist, but explore means by which present authoritarian governments can pave the way for democratic regimes, by:

    a. Encouraging firm observance of rule of law.

    b. Assisting Asians to understand democratic political processes and to find a realistic, honest way to finance an orderly and vigorous party system.

    c. Assisting officer corps to acquire administrative and managerial skills necessary in new political tasks they are assuming.

   2. Encourage Southeast Asian countries to coordinate educational and economic needs and to direct educational efforts at producing a literate and vocationally trained population, rather than uprooted semi-intellectuals lacking opportunity for jobs they consider suitable.

B. ECONOMIC. U.S. should:

   1. Cooperate with other Western nations to develop concrete long-range development programs which are not simply economic plans but which carefully consider political, administrative, and social factors.

   2. Encourage and assist efforts to increase long-range food production by:

      a. Fostering greatly increased capital formation in the form of land development, irrigation, roads, etc.

      b. Promoting agrarian reform and revolutionary changes in such institutions as marketing, credit, and state aid to peasantry.

      c. Endeavoring to harmonize rice-culture interests of southeast Asian countries.

   3. Explore and encourage ways and means to achieve eventual economic and cultural integration.

C. MILITARY. U.S. should:

   1. *Not* rely on defense arrangements in highly unstable countries, but should foster constructive action programs to enable these countries to resist Communism internally as well as externally.

   2. *Not* regard SEATO as an efficient instrumentality for achieving economic and social consolidation; SEATO's anti-subversive activities, however, may profitably be pursued in the short run.

IV. RECOMMENDED U.S. POLICIES TOWARD NORTHEAST ASIA.

A. JAPAN.

   1. Political. U.S. should:

      a. Develop deeper intellectual, political, and cultural roots for U.S.-Japanese alliance.

      (1) U.S. cultural relations with Japanese masses should be improved by increasing selective personal contacts between Americans and Japanese of same occupations and by making U.S. popular literature and entertainment more accessible to Japanese common man.

      (2) Because Japan is an elitist society, U.S. should direct part of its cultural relations programs toward Japanese leaders.

      (3) U.S. officials should have broader and more extensive contacts with Japanese society.

Conlon

    b. Propose Japan (and India) for permanent membership in U.N. Security Council when and if changes are contemplated by U.N.

2. Economic. U.S. should:

    a. Improve U.S.-Japanese economic relations by:

      (1) Resisting domestic pressures in U.S. for higher tariffs against Japan.

      (2) Exploring what bilateral and multilateral organizations might improve U.S.-Japanese economic relations.

      (3) Urging Japan to take appropriate actions to improve her trade with U.S.

        (a) Step up and better supervise small and medium export industries.

        (b) Diversify exports and give greater support to industrial research.

        (c) Undertake more scientific studies of U.S. market.

        (d) Improve investment climate and conditions for foreign business in Japan.

    b. Foster U.S.-Japanese cooperation to promote economic development in non-Communist Asia by:

      (1) Contributing jointly to international institutions or funds providing credit facilities.

      (2) Supporting organizations seeking some control over prices and production of primary goods in area.

      (3) Giving joint technical financial assistance on specific products.

      (4) Reaching some collective agreement on problems of international fishing grounds and conservation of fishing resources.

    c. Seek to provide Japan with sufficient outlets for her goods in the West to minimize attractiveness of Chinese markets.

3. Military. U.S. should:

    a. Avoid pressing Japan for rapid rearmament under present conditions.

    b. Maintain bases in Japan for time being, but consider in the long range whether it will be desirable for U.S. to maintain large network of bases in populous areas of East Asia.

B. OKINAWA. U.S. should:

1. Accept necessity of Okinawa's eventual reversion to Japan and develop plans now to take account of timing and adjustment needed to insure long-range U.S. interests.

2. Use civilian rather than military administration during the interim adjustment period.

3. Give economic assistance of type proposed in the Price bill.

C. KOREA. U.S. should:

1. Foster maintenance of democratic rights by:

    a. Giving greater coverage to Korean politics in American press.

78

    b. Making clear to all political groups that good U.S.-Korean relations depend on Korean maintenance of basic rights—and using sanctions, if necessary, to back up this warning.

2. Encourage improved Korean diplomatic, cultural, economic relations with the non-Communist world.

    a. Give special attention to improving Korean-Japanese relations, devoting serious thought to possible compromise solutions which U.S. might propose privately and underwrite.

3. Encourage all types of cultural relations and mutual scholarship.

4. Reassess U.S. aid policies with regard to following questions:

    a. What form of aid is most conducive to developing Korean efforts and capital formation?

    b. To what extent should U.S. aid be geared to long-range plans, and what should be U.S. responsibility for checking validity and progress of plans?

    c. What is best balance between military and economic aid? Cannot military expenditures of Korean government be reduced?

D. COMMUNIST CHINA AND TAIWAN. U.S. should:

1. Base its policies on these realities:

    a. Communist Chinese regime will likely have a long life (barring a major war).

    b. The Sino-Soviet alliance will not be ruptured easily and will probably endure for a considerable period, although Sino-Soviet mutual interests are likely to decrease with the passage of time.

    c. Communist China is likely to emerge as one of major world powers of the late twentieth century, although it will continue some dependence on the Soviet Union.

    d. Communist China is already participating actively and increasingly in international affairs; the main question is whether she can be persuaded or forced to bear any responsibility for her participation.

2. Pursue a three-stage policy of exploration and negotiation.

    a. The objectives of this policy would be:

        (1) To test the willingness of Communist China to coexist with us.

        (2) To seek a more dynamic, flexible and positive policy, although one with certain firm commitments.

        (3) To make possible greater collective agreement on the China issue among major free world nations.

    b. Three stages would be followed, each stage being contingent on the success of the preceding one.

        (1) Exchange of journalists, scholars, commercial representatives with Communist China; an attempt to have informal discussions between Communist Chinese leaders and some prominent American individual or group not in Executive Branch of U.S.

government; informal, private discussions on China problem
between U.S., allies, Japan, some "neutrals."

(2) Abandonment of CHINCOM restrictions and permission
for trade with China on same basis as that with the U.S.S.R.;
informal discussion with allies and "neutrals" on admission of
Communist China to U.N. and of newly recognized Republic of
Taiwan to U.N. General Assembly and on enlargement of
Security Council to include India and Japan as well as China as
permanent members; simultaneous discussions with our small
allies pledging full and continued support to all our treaty obligations, particularly those to Taiwan, to whom pledges of expanded economic-technical assistance would also be made. U.S.
would, in addition, try to help resettle mainland refugees who
want to leave Taiwan.

(3) Negotiation of a U.S. commercial treaty with Communist
China and, *if* this is successful, de facto recognition of her.

3. Withdraw in any case from the offshore islands.

Study No. 6

THE OPERATIONAL ASPECTS OF U.S. FOREIGN POLICY

Maxwell Graduate School of
Citizenship and Public Affairs
Syracuse University
Syracuse, New York

Published: November 11, 1959

GOALS OF THE REPORT

1. *To recommend* U.S. approaches toward the profound changes occurring in international affairs.
2. *To suggest* administrative and organizational reforms required to cope with these changes.

MAJOR PREMISES OF THE REPORT

1. The U.S. is involved in the internal affairs of other nations to an unprecedented extent.
2. The U.S. must accept involvement as a permanent fact of its international life and must use it constructively.
3. In underdeveloped areas U.S. foreign policy should work toward economic progress while also fostering responsible governments—governments that rule by consent and are reasonably responsive to the mass needs.

I. RECOMMENDED U.S. APPROACHES TOWARD THE PROFOUND CHANGES OCCURRING IN INTERNATIONAL AFFAIRS.

A. WESTERN EUROPE. The U.S. must continue to encourage:

1. Western Europe's dramatic economic growth.
2. European integration.
3. Increased European participation in programs to modernize less developed areas.

B. THE UNDERDEVELOPED AREAS. U.S. must:

1. Firmly support nationalism as an avowed U.S. policy, particularly in those areas where nationalism is among the strongest social emotions. For example:
   a. Although America generally favors expanding the private industrial sector of underdeveloped countries, the U.S. should abandon open avowal of such a policy in countries where that sector of the economy is controlled by foreigners.
   b. Although U.S. relationships with Western allies prevent our adopting a policy of indiscriminately supporting immediate independence of colonies, U.S. should not participate in relationships between the metropoles and their colonies.
   c. The U.S. should concentrate its economic aid and other efforts in those countries already independent.

2. Promote democracy as a legitimate aim of U.S. foreign policy.
   a. The U.S. must recognize that democracy is a flexible concept.
   b. It should accept as "democratic" any form of government that is responsible, rules by consent, and is reasonably responsive to the needs of the people.
3. U.S. must accept, and in some instances even encourage, the neutrality or non-alignment of underdeveloped nations in the cold war. The existence of a sizable "uncommitted" group of nations can serve as a powerful force in reducing international tensions.
4. Vigorously promote economic development as a necessity if these countries are not to seek in desperation Communism as a means of abolishing poverty. In promoting economic development, the U.S. must:
   a. Tolerate forms of economic enterprise different from our own. In particular, U.S. must understand the need for some governments to exercise considerable control over their economies.
   b. Accept the fact that U.S. action, or inaction, involves America in other nations' internal affairs.
   c. Be willing to continue its economic aid programs for periods measured in decades rather than years.

C. THE COMMUNIST BLOC.

1. The challenge of Soviet production.
   a. U.S. should react to the rapid growth of Soviet heavy industrial production by working toward a vigorous, fully employed economy:
      (1) Eliminating the waste resulting from cyclical recessions.
      (2) Firmly resisting all forms of "creeping protectionism."
   b. The Soviet political and military advantages accruing from their industrial growth should be countered by:
      (1) Wise use of present U.S. resources to foster technological and scientific breakthroughs, and
      (2) Promotion of economic development in non-Communist underdeveloped areas.
2. The challenge of Soviet aid and trade policies.
   a. U.S. must not overestimate political effects of Soviet economic aid.
   b. U.S. must not adopt a policy of hostility toward countries that accept Soviet loans and trade offers. To prevent these countries from being victimized by Soviet economic pressure, U.S. must be willing to cushion economic blows if Soviet aid and trade are withdrawn.
3. Eastern European satellites. U.S. should:
   a. Encourage trade relations and cultural exchange between Eastern Europe and the non-Communist world.

b. Support efforts of the satellites to control their own destinies within limits tolerable to the U.S.S.R.

4. Communist China.

   a. Recognizing the Chinese Communist regime should not be the central question of U.S. policy; U.S. must focus instead on China's growing power.

   b. U.S. must concentrate on economic development of non-Communist Asia to serve as an economic and ideological counterweight to China.

D. THE MILITARY STAND-OFF.

1. Diplomacy, and other non-violent aspects of foreign policy, must play a greater role in U.S. security arrangements. (The military is becoming a less usable instrument of policy as the weaponry designed for less than total war becomes more dangerous to use.)

2. The network of U.S. bases overseas can be drastically reduced during the 1960's because of the development of intercontinental ballistic missiles and missile-carrying submarines.

   a. Plans should be laid now to minimize economic dislocations and fully exploit the political opportunities resulting from our withdrawal.

   b. Such bases as are needed for the pre-positioning of troops and supplies for limited war situations should be moved to areas where the bases will provoke minimal political friction.

3. U.S. military alliances outside the NATO area should be replaced by looser regional arrangements which can include nations unwilling to participate in formal military commitments.

4. Limitation and control of armaments must be an active goal of U.S.

   a. U.S. must have a permanent policy of keeping disarmament negotiations continuously active by the frequent introduction of new, workable proposals.

   b. An appropriate institution should be created within the U.S. foreign policy complex to develop a continuing disarmament policy.

II. THREE IMPORTANT OBJECTIVES OF U.S. FOREIGN POLICY AND THE MEANS RECOMMENDED FOR ACHIEVING THEM.

A. WORK WITH THE "NEXT GOVERNMENT" IN A FOREIGN COUNTRY, not just the regime of the date. To achieve this objective the U.S. must:

1. Effectively keep in touch with every element of local power in every country to which we have access.

    a. Official U.S. contacts with forces likely to be in power in the future are facilitated by our wide-ranging economic assistance programs and by our programs for providing weapons and training of military personnel.

    b. The many non-official Americans abroad—businessmen, missionaries, etc.—can make even wider and deeper contacts. This web of communications should be given greater encouragement and used more by U.S. officials.

2. Concentrate major foreign operations on institutions and programs which promise to survive the transitory ambitions of individual regimes.

    a. U.S. must analyze the political and social side-effects of its programs and design its operations so the changes they induce will be desirable ones. The U.S., for example, should support:

    (1) *Land reform programs.* U.S. should commit a sizable sum each year to help reorganize land use in underdeveloped areas and should entrust to the U.N. the working out of detailed plans for the use of these funds.

    (2) *U.S. aid to schools and colleges.* Educational programs must also be accompanied by activities which provide work for the newly educated youngsters.

    (3) *Health and birth control programs.* To minimize domestic political pressures the U.S. should approach birth control through international organizations.

    (4) *Military training operations.* The role of the military in political change in many countries suggests employing instructors with special understanding of civil government and with special training in the cultural history, etc., of the countries concerned.

    b. The following overall policies should be followed in U.S. aid programs.

    (1) Avoidance of "shadow projects" designed primarily to benefit groups in power.

    (2) Emphasis on a few long-term programs of major significance rather than a host of miscellaneous small projects.

    (3) Channeling as much aid as possible through multilateral organizations.

        (a) When astutely managed, multilateral organizations can become deeply involved in the touchiest "domestic" decisions of member countries without raising issues of national sovereignty.

        (b) A multilateral approach should stimulate and serve to coordinate the contributions of other industrial nations to economic development programs.

B. **PARTICIPATE EFFECTIVELY IN THE REVOLUTIONARY PROCESSES OF ECONOMIC DEVELOPMENT.** To do this the U.S. must contribute much more capital to development.

1. $3-4 billion of additional capital could be utilized each year by the less developed countries, and annual absorptive capacity will increase over the next ten years.

2. To supply the needed capital, the U.S. should, at least for the next decade, devote to economic development ¼ of the yearly increase in U.S. gross national product. This would be over and above present levels of aid.

3. Current reductions in U.S. gold stocks should not deter U.S. from dramatic increases in aid programs.

   a. U.S. still has adequate gold reserves in comparison with the volume of U.S. international trade.

   b. The imbalance in U.S. foreign payments is not properly corrected by reducing U.S. aid. Increase of U.S. exports, through vigorous action by U.S. businessmen, and reduction or elimination of the many remaining barriers to U.S. exports, particularly in Western Europe, is called for.

   c. U.S. should not resort to "tied loans" in its aid programs as a means of increasing its exports.

4. U.S. surplus agricultural commodities are a source of capital for underdeveloped areas

   a. U.S. could enter into long-term agreements (5 to 10 years) to provide surplus commodities at either fixed or world-market prices.

   b. Other countries exporting these same agricultural commodities might join in some of these agreements.

   c. The recipients of these commodities would be able to devote their limited resources to non-agricultural projects rather than emphasizing food production at all costs.

5. Foreign currencies accumulated by the U.S. cannot add significantly to the capital requirements of economic development.

   a. These funds do not add real resources to the U.S.

   b. Local currencies, however, may be applied to useful and important activities, including educational exchange. (If carefully managed, they can add somewhat to the internal resources devoted to capital formation.)

C. **FOSTER REGIONAL GROUPINGS AND INSTITUTIONS.** To support this goal different approaches must be used in different areas.

1. *Western Europe:* U.S. should support the Common Market through private investment, expanded trade, and political encouragement.

2. *Latin America:* U.S. should encourage British and Common Market participation in the economic development of the region.

3. *South and Southeast Asia:* U.S. should foster some form of regional development organization, staffed and operated primarily by Asians, particularly from India and Japan, but with enough participation by others to avoid the appearance of substituting Indian and Japanese imperialism for that of the white West.

4. *Middle East:* U.S. should help set in motion the Arab Financial Institution, already in an advanced planning stage.

5. *Africa:* U.S. should foster federations of the small states and encourage a regional approach to some of the problems common to all emerging ex-colonies.

III. SUGGESTED CHANGES IN THE ADMINISTRATION OF U.S. FOREIGN AFFAIRS.

A. CREATION OF A MULTILATERAL ORGANIZATION FOR GLOBAL COORDINATION OF ECONOMIC DEVELOPMENT PROGRAMS.

1. A global Development Authority, under U.N. auspices, should be established with:
   a. Clear-cut responsibility for defining the overall objectives and operating principles to be followed by the various international development agencies.
   b. Consistent policy and management, not subject to arbitrary pressures in favor of particular national interests or viewpoints and with full authority to select and supervise its own staff.
   c. Strong support of its member countries.

2. A strong field director in each country would be responsible to the global authority. The field director should be empowered to:
   a. Work out, with the local authorities, a realistic national development program for the country. (Most of the less developed countries do not have the technical skills or administrative machinery to do such programming without outside help.)
   b. On the basis of this program recommend which projects or types of projects should receive allocation of international funds.
   c. Coordinate the local operations of the various international agencies.

3. Regional organizations, such as the Inter-American Bank, would serve as an intermediate agency between the country directors and the global authority for reviewing and coordinating programs and allocating funds.

B. REORGANIZATION OF U.S. GOVERNMENT OPERATIONS OVERSEAS.

1. In all U.S. overseas operations, genuine delegation of responsible authority to the field is necessary for flexible, effective administration.

2. The U.S. ambassador in each country should not only perform the normal diplomatic functions (negotiating, reporting, etc.) but should also preside over the whole range of U.S. governmental activities in the country of his assignment.

   a. To fulfill this role the ambassador must have executive as well as diplomatic ability of the first order.

      (1) The U.S. may sometimes have to look beyond the career foreign service for the executive ability required of a U.S. ambassador, but national political party leaders should endorse only those political candidates for embassy service who have already had successful executive and international service.

      (2) The pool of potential executives for future ambassadorial assignments can be enlarged within the Foreign Service by:

         (a) Widening the Foreign Service to take in more "generalists" from International Cooperation Administration (ICA) and U.S. Information Agency (USIA).

         (b) Insuring that members of such a combined Foreign Service have a variety of assignments during their careers including opportunities to work in a foreign aid program.

   b. The ambassador would direct all bilateral U.S. aid operations in the country of his assignment and would keep a sharp eye on the operation of multilateral aid programs.

3. U.S. representatives to multilateral agencies should normally be career diplomats because of the diplomatic skill required in such posts.

4. Some shifts of emphasis in U.S. higher education would help develop the skills needed in Americans working abroad.

   a. Colleges and universities should make it a live option for every interested student to spend at least a semester abroad under competent academic supervision.

   b. University area and language programs should be expanded and should offer their regular students a brief but intensive exposure to one country.

   c. Curriculum changes should be made in every professional school and graduate program in the social sciences in recognition of the fact that some of the students will practice their professions abroad.

C. REORGANIZATION OF WASHINGTON OFFICES DEALING WITH FOREIGN AFFAIRS.

1. The Secretary of State should be the President's chief of staff for coordination of the foreign policy aspects of all government activity (including such difficult cases as the Defense Department, the budget process, the setting of monetary, loan and tariff policy, and the disposal of agricultural surpluses).

   a. This function should not be assigned to some new office separate from and above the State Department.

   b. Consider making the Secretary of State Executive Vice Chairman of the National Security Council.

2. An effective policy-planning staff should be developed to aid the Secretary of State.

   a. A cadre of trained policy thinkers should be developed through assignment of promising Foreign Service officers to policy planning in Washington or major foreign embassies for a larger-than-average share of their duty tours.

3. USIA and ICA should be kept separate from the State Department to reduce the administrative burdens of the Secretary of State.

4. ICA and DLF should be combined.

5. The various U.S. aid operations should be administered as follows:

   a. Military aid should be administered bilaterally through the Defense Department.

   b. Defense support should be administered bilaterally by ICA.

   c. Economic assistance to countries having special security or other political importance (e.g., Jordan, Korea) should be administered bilaterally by ICA.

   d. General economic development programs should be placed under multilateral administration as far as possible, but should be reviewed by the combined ICA-DLF. Until acceptable international machinery for such administration is established these programs would be administered by ICA-DLF.

6. A select joint committee of Congress, broadly representative of party and committee leadership in both Houses, should make a careful study of the proper role and organization of Congress in the conduct of foreign affairs.

Study No. 7

BASIC AIMS OF U.S. FOREIGN POLICY

Council on Foreign Relations,
Inc.
58 East 68th Street
New York, New York

Published: November 25, 1959

GOALS OF THE REPORT

1. *To analyze* the basic aims of U.S. foreign policy.
2. *To estimate* the extent to which these aims are supported by the American people.
3. *To project* the future role the United States should play in order to achieve its basic aims.

MAJOR PREMISES OF THE REPORT

1. Foreign policy formulation must include calculations of national interest in specific circumstances; only rarely can it correspond fully to broad statements of aim and principle.
2. Although there are inevitable limits to what foreign policy can achieve, the means and opportunities for U.S. leadership could be more fully used than in the past.
3. However, the formulation of long-range goals is an absolute prerequisite to the adequate conduct of foreign policy.
4. Future opportunities and difficulties for U.S. foreign policy will be of such magnitude as to demand a considerable increase in U.S. efforts. To achieve its foreign policy aims the U.S. and the free world must achieve positions of increased economic, political and military strength.

I. MAJOR AIMS AND PRINCIPLES OF U.S. FOREIGN POLICY PRIOR TO WORLD WAR I.

A. HISTORIC U.S. POLICIES AND PRINCIPLES IN COMMON WITH WESTERN COMMUNITY.

1. Freedom of the seas.
2. Free exchange of ideas.
3. Freedom for citizens to trade and do business abroad without discrimination.
4. Respect for international obligations.
5. Conduct of international relations through techniques of negotiation, arbitration and judicial settlement.

B. HISTORIC U.S. POLICIES AND PRINCIPLES UNIQUE IN THE WESTERN COMMUNITY.

1. U.S. insistence that outside powers refrain from establishing themselves in the Western Hemisphere (Monroe Doctrine).

2. Calculated aloofness from the conflicts and alliances of the great powers of Europe.
3. Indifference to extending influence overseas.
4. Moral support for the right of all peoples to individual and national freedom. This "made the U.S. a revolutionary influence in the world of that time."

II. MAJOR CHANGES IN U.S. FOREIGN POLICY AIMS AND ENVIRONMENT SINCE WORLD WAR I.

A. MAJOR CHANGES IN U.S. FOREIGN POLICY *AIMS* SINCE WORLD WAR I.

1. To extend U.S. influence abroad.
2. To promote political self-determination for overseas areas.
3. To engage in collective arrangements through regional and world organizations as a means to national security.
4. To pursue policies consonant with new U.S. recognition of military and economic interdependence with other nations.

B. MAJOR CHANGES IN U.S. FOREIGN *ENVIRONMENT* SINCE WORLD WAR II.

1. Onset of Sino-Soviet expansionism.
2. Political and economic recovery of Western Europe.
3. Political and economic revolution in less-developed areas.
4. U.S.-Soviet development of nuclear weapons.
5. Growth of major scientific and technological achievement.

III. ASSESSMENT OF U.S. FOREIGN POLICY PERFORMANCE SINCE WORLD WAR II.

A. U.S. HAS A CREDITABLE RECORD of having made, at critical points, major decisions which were "bold in conception and salutary in their effect," e.g., the Marshall Plan, the Truman Doctrine for Greece and Turkey, U.S. action in Korea in 1950. This record has created the outlines of a national strategy.

B. U.S. HAS BEEN LARGELY SUCCESSFUL IN RESISTING COMMUNIST EXPANSION.

C. THE DEMANDS OF THE COLD WAR, however, have obscured other challenges bound to affect our world position and have also tended to divert us from formulating long-term policies.

D. RECENT U.S. POLICIES INSIDE THE FREE WORLD could have been more dynamic and positive despite necessity to exercise our international leadership through mutual consent.

E. OVERALL U.S. POLICY HAS BEEN "CRISIS-ORIENTED" and deficient in long-range planning.

   1. Some reasons for this are:
     a. Defective policy-making machinery.
     b. U.S. Constitution's division of foreign policy responsibility between the Executive and Legislative branches of government, and the resultant tendency to tie "policies and programs to the Procrustean inflexibility of the fiscal year."

   2. This can and must change:
     a. Defects in policy-making machinery can be corrected.
     b. The traditional division of powers does not preclude cooperation or prevent either branch from developing fruitful ideas and approaches.
     c. Present conditions are as favorable to initiatives on the part of free nations as they are to those of the Soviet Union or to Communist China.
     d. A prerequisite to developing initiatives is a change in attitudes, foresight and leadership within the American body politic.

IV. THE FOREIGN POLICY TASKS WHICH LIE AHEAD.

The U.S. must strive to:

A. BUILD A NEW INTERNATIONAL ORDER. The new international order, rather than seeking to maintain the status quo, must be responsive to world aspirations for peace, for social and economic change, and for liberation from alien domination. To accomplish this the U.S. must:

   1. Search for an international order in which the freedom of nations is recognized as interdependent and in which many policies are jointly undertaken by free world states with differing political, economic and social systems, and including states labeling themselves as "socialist."
   2. Safeguard U.S. security through preserving a system of bilateral agreements and regional arrangements.
   3. Maintain and gradually increase the authority of the U.N.
   4. Make more effective use of the International Court of Justice, jurisdiction of which should be increased by withdrawal of reservations by member nations on matters judged to be domestic.

B. PROMOTE THE SOLIDARITY OF THE ATLANTIC COMMUNITY (Western Europe and Western Hemisphere). The U.S. must:

   1. Maintain and strengthen the Community's security organizations (NATO and OAS) and, using a flexible approach, develop such

new organizations as may be necessary for such other purposes as economic cooperation.

2. Strive to prevent the crystallization of conflicting blocs within the Atlantic Community.

3. Prevent Atlantic Community solidarity from becoming (or seeming to become) a front against non-Western nations.

C. ASSIST THE LESS-DEVELOPED AREAS. It is in the interest of the entire free world to have some of the less-developed countries, soon, reach the point of breakthrough to self-sustained development.

1. U.S. economic aid programs must be more ambitious, longer term, and aimed at specific areas and tasks. U.S. efforts, supplemented by those of Western Europe and Japan, should aim to:
   a. Increase considerably the amount of capital goods flowing from industrial to less-developed countries.
   b. Foster development of technical and administrative competence in less-developed countries.
   c. Correct or minimize the effects of drastic swings in the prices of certain basic commodities (particularly in Latin America).
   d. Tackle the population problem in areas of rapid growth before it reaches disastrous proportions.

2. U.S. economic aid programs should *avoid:*
   a. Making substantial increases contingent upon the freeing of funds resulting from disarmament agreements.
   b. Making aid contingent upon political commitments to the West.
   c. Committing us to absolute choices between European colonial powers and their dependencies. We must promote a peaceful transformation of the relationship between each of these groups to mitigate or prevent such dilemmas.
   d. Any flavor of neo-colonialism. U.S. should offer less-developed nations partnerships more appealing than "partnership" with the Communist bloc.

3. U.S. should generally favor multinational approaches to foreign aid.
   a. Such approaches will:
      (1) Increase the magnitude of the total effort.
      (2) Make it easier to tackle economic problems on their merits without wounding the sensibilities of aid-recipients.
      (3) Blunt the damaging political effects of Communist bilateral programs.
   b. Bilateral programs would continue to be useful in some instances.
   c. A long-term program should be devised in an international forum to help solve the world's food supply problems with the help of American agricultural surpluses.

D. MEET THE COMMUNIST MILITARY CHALLENGE. Military power is a prerequisite to, but not a substitute for, an effective foreign policy.

    1. Basic U.S. military requirements are:

        a. Retaliatory power sufficient to make the cost of launching a major attack on the free world unacceptable to Communist leadership.

        b. Mobile forces capable of coping with limited war situations.

        c. A research and development program to insure maximum progress in militarily useful scientific and technological projects.

        d. A long-range global military aid program to strengthen U.S. and allied defenses.

    2. There are "serious doubts" as to whether these basic requirements are being fully met now. But it is imperative that they be met firmly and with whatever sacrifice is necessary.

E. CONDUCT SERIOUS NEGOTIATIONS TO ACHIEVE INTERNATIONAL AGREEMENT ON LIMITATION, REDUCTION, AND CONTROL OF ARMAMENTS. A negative or perfunctory approach by the U.S. would compromise U.S. influence abroad and jeopardize the achievement of our foreign policy aims.

    1. The U.S. should simultaneously explore every avenue:

        a. Fully explore Soviet proposals for complete or partial disarmament.

        b. Concentrate more on developing our own disarmament proposals.

        c. Negotiate on these problems perhaps directly with the U.S.S.R., in secret, but not neglecting consultations with our major allies.

        d. Negotiate in the framework of the U.N.

    2. U.S. action in this field should be guided by these facts:

        a. The new international order the U.S. should seek to build cannot be dominated by an uncontrolled arms race.

        b. Significant progress in the control of arms demands a genuine commitment to the concept of collective security and the development of a stronger international political structure.

        c. Although disarmament cannot rest on paper promises incapable of enforcement, the inevitable risks accompanying any proposed armament limitation and control should be weighed against the risks of failure to make any progress at all.

        d. Efforts to resolve political conflicts with Communist powers should occur simultaneous with, NOT prior to disarmament negotiations.

F. NEGOTIATE WITH THE COMMUNISTS ON SUCH ISSUES AS GERMANY, in hope of finding mutually acceptable arrangements, if only limited and partial ones.

1. The importance of acceptable agreements on such questions as disarmament and Germany is such that a continuing reappraisal of the possibilities and probing of the adversary's positions is necessary.
2. Channels must exist to communicate with the Communist regimes, including that of Communist China. "In general, the most promising channels for communication with the Soviet Union and Communist China will be regular or *ad hoc* contacts maintaining the necessary conditions of true negotiation, which may at times be at the highest level, but not public performances of ministers or heads of government."
3. To negotiate successfully the U.S. and the free world must be in a position of military, political, and economic strength.

V. THE ROLE OF THE AMERICAN PEOPLE IN U.S. FOREIGN POLICY.

A. THE AMERICAN PEOPLE PARTICIPATE IN FOREIGN POLICY THROUGH THEIR INFLUENCE ON THE REST OF THE WORLD. The impact of America on most other nations is made not solely or even primarily by official diplomacy but by:

1. The massive contact between peoples and cultures characteristic of this age.
2. The conduct of American society and the resultant image of America projected abroad.

B. THE AMERICAN PEOPLE PARTICIPATE IN FOREIGN POLICY THROUGH THEIR INFLUENCE ON THE POLICIES OF THEIR OWN GOVERNMENT and the support they give those policies.

1. The government must be generally responsive to public opinion, but it works under a great handicap if the public is ill informed on the significant issues or if political leaders choose to play domestic politics with them.
2. *It is, however, imperative that there be effective leadership,* particularly at the Presidential level, to give voice to our national purpose and to persuade the people of the need to make greater efforts and sacrifices to meet both immediate and distant goals.

Study No. 8

DEVELOPMENTS IN MILITARY TECHNOLOGY AND THEIR INFLUENCE ON U.S. STRATEGY AND FOREIGN POLICY

Washington Center of Foreign
  Policy Research
The Johns Hopkins University
1906 Florida Avenue, N.W.
Washington, D. C.

Published: December 6, 1959

GOALS OF THE REPORT

1. *To analyze* anticipated developments in military technology during the next decade in terms of:
   a. Their implications for U.S. military strategy.
   b. Their relationship to U.S. foreign policy aims.
2. *To suggest* revisions of U.S. military policy which become advisable in light of anticipated military technology developments.

MAJOR PREMISES OF THE REPORT

1. The overriding objective of U.S. foreign policy should be to promote and secure world conditions compatible with purposes of U.S. and free world.
   a. The U.S. will necessarily pursue this objective amid Soviet efforts to build a world order on opposing principles.
   b. The objective demands a protracted U.S. effort, designed to cope with a variety of possible Soviet threats.
2. Adequate and appropriate U.S. military strength is the precondition of free world security.
3. A defense policy designed to prevent Sino-Soviet encroachments on the free world is essential to U.S. foreign policy for as long as the cold war continues.
4. Technological development of strategic weaponry has reduced the number of major military powers to two—U.S. and U.S.S.R.
5. The principle of collective defense has become basic to U.S. military security because the U.S. cannot rely solely on its own resources or solely on the capacities of the U.N.

I. U.S. NATIONAL PURPOSES AND STRATEGY.

A. TO PROMOTE INTERNATIONAL ORDER COMPATIBLE WITH VALUES OF FREE WORLD.

1. Two world wars and spread of modern technology shattered traditional world order built on the European balance of power and cast to the fore the U.S. and hostile U.S.S.R.
2. After World War II, the U.S. recognized its interests and security were dependent on an international system, with the U.S. providing a major source of strength:
   a. Which permits or provides for cooperation in many forms—bilateral, regional, or multilateral, for example:
      (1) Economic: International Monetary Fund, World Bank, General Agreement on Tariffs and Trade

(2) Military: North Atlantic Treaty Organization, Southeast Asia Treaty Organization

(3) Political: United Nations, Organization of American States.

   b. Which allies diverse systems and interests of the entire non-Communist world and gives hope to those who wish to weaken ties with the Communist bloc (e.g.; Yugoslavia, Poland).

B. DEFENSE AGAINST COMMUNIST EXPANSION.

1. Increased competition with the Soviet Union in years following World War II forced the U.S. to relate foreign policy increasingly to military strength, causing:
   a. Greater defense expenditures.
   b. Greater emphasis on military rather than economic aid.
   c. Tendency to choose allies because of the contribution they could make to collective defense.
2. Responsible leadership precludes a Fortress America retreat or preventive war, and demands heavy, long-term commitment, at once creative and defensive.

II. U.S. DEFENSE POLICY.

A. SHIFT TO COLLECTIVE DEFENSE POLICY FOLLOWING WORLD WAR II.

1. The U.S. entered the worldwide collective security organization, the U.N., and
2. Developed regional security alliances outside the U.N. (NATO, SEATO, CENTO) when the cold war raised doubts about the effectiveness of the U.N.
   a. Premise: American independence and way of life would be imperiled by Communist control of Eurasia, which neither the U.S. nor the free world could alone prevent.
   b. Defense against Sino-Soviet aggression entailed:
      (1) Greatly widening our defense perimeter including practically all areas not already in the Sino-Soviet orbit.
      (2) Commitment to containment rather than aggression.
      (3) Provision of U.S. economic and military aid to participating nations.
3. Collective military effort must be great enough to guard against strategic nuclear attack and a wide variety of nonnuclear threats.
4. Collective defense requires consideration of many nonmilitary matters, e.g.:
   a. Internal politics of allies (regime may demand excessive military aid or even abandonment of bases).
   b. Geographical factors (deployment of forces over a vast area).
   c. Frictions among nuclear "haves" and "have-nots."

    d. Feuds peripheral to cold war (Israel-Arab, India-Pakistan, France-Algeria, etc.).

    e. Possible need of newly-independent areas for military assistance to offset Soviet offers of aid, and to forestall "indirect" aggression.

B. MAINTENANCE OF BALANCE OF STRATEGIC POWER.

1. Technological achievements of the Soviet Union by 1957 threatened a shift of the strategic balance of power to their favor.

2. "Balance of strategic power" (or nuclear stalemate) exists when neither side can expect its first offensive to sufficiently cripple the other's retaliatory capacity. It is determined by:

    a. Technological factors (performance of weapons).

    b. Non-technological forces (geographic size, natural resources, population, military manpower, quality of strategic thought, willingness to take initiative, etc.). U.S. has superior industrial capacity, but may be endangered by Soviet advantages due to:

      (1) Greater emphasis on heavy industrial investment at the expense of consumer production.

      (2) Shorter time-lag between weapons research and production.

      (3) Greater military intelligence and secrecy.

      (4) Possession of the initiative to strike (since the free world is unwilling to be an aggressor).

3. Development of nuclear weapons to date has changed the character of the world military balance, by:

    a. Replacing a multinational system with a bipolar one.

    b. Leaving neither U.S. nor U.S.S.R. with a decisive military advantage.

    c. Making assessment of the balance of military power vastly difficult.

    d. Heightening military insecurity by a weapons revolution which has developed through three stages:

      (1) Conventional—which ended shortly after World War II.

      (2) Nuclear—U.S. believed its supremacy in strategic airpower could deter Soviet attack even after the U.S. learned that the Soviets were stockpiling hydrogen bombs and had developed long-range jets.

      (3) Nuclear-missile:

        (a) The successful Soviet ICBM test in 1957 and the launching of two earth satellites made the U.S. consider the possibility of a Soviet first-strike against the Strategic Air Command (SAC).

        (b) U.S. tried to protect SAC through dispersal, broader alert status, and anti-air defense technology (radar jammers, etc.).

4. Present "missile gap" period holds gravest immediate danger for the U.S. due to:
   a. Soviet strategic striking power with the growing ability to make a successful first-strike against our strategic forces.
   b. Soviet missile lead, as yet uncompensated for by the U.S. missile warning systems, and possible Soviet intelligence advantages.
   c. Comparative inadequacy of U.S. civil defense system.
5. Later reliance on ICBM's holds possibility of greater military stability.
   a. Greater numbers, increased mobility, cover, concealment and dispersal of missiles will reduce the effectiveness of a single surprise attack and increase the value of missile deterrent.
   b. Surprise—or first-strike—attack will demand much greater expenditure of resources by aggressor.
      (1) Aggressor must strike at protected strategic forces.
      (2) Retaliator need only be able to inflict unacceptable losses on more vulnerable population and industrial centers.
6. Factors opposing present stabilizing influence of nuclear retaliatory capability (even a small number of retaliatory weapons can rob victory of any appeal) are:
   a. Vulnerability of striking systems which raise danger of surprise attack.
   b. Timing of nuclear developments (i.e., country may decide to strike if it thinks it has the lead).
   c. Policy instabilities due to the use of war threats.
   d. Spread of nuclear weapons capabilities to other nations.
   e. Defense weaknesses (making for susceptibility to surprise attack) and "hair-trigger" warning systems with danger of war by accident.
   f. Possible non-enforceable total disarmament agreement.
7. Anticipated technological developments should not upset present nuclear stability.
   a. Forseeable weapon developments do not promise to upset present military balance.
   b. Technological developments will tend to favor deterrer. The increased number and diversity of retaliatory weapons will undermine the confidence of an aggressor in its ability to destroy them.
   c. Increasing cost and complexity of weapons system will more and more limit major military status to the U.S. and the U.S.S.R. and feed divisive influences in presently existing alliance systems.
   d. Improvements in warheads and delivery systems, however, will make it possible to initiate war with increasing speed and decisiveness.
   e. Increased air and ground mobility and greater firepower for lower echelons of the military may mean more rapid initiation, or termination of limited or localized conflicts.

III. NEED FOR WIDER RANGE OF MILITARY CAPABILITIES.

A. GROWING SOVIET STRATEGIC POWER HAS MADE U.S. "MASSIVE RETALIATION" THREAT LESS EFFECTIVE means of protecting our overseas allies.

   1. Reliance on the threat of nuclear retaliation has discouraged European development of the means to meet limited aggression.
   2. U.S. itself has dangerously limited its forces for deterrence or defeat of limited aggression.

B. LACK OF EFFECTIVE ALTERNATIVE TO NUCLEAR THREAT IS A PRIMARY WEAKNESS OF U.S. DEFENSE CAPABILITY at a time when the risks involved have made U.S. nuclear retaliation less likely in event of:

   1. Nonnuclear aggression against allies.
   2. Tactical nuclear aggression.
   3. Aggression in areas where U.S. interests are held to be less than vital.

C. U.S., NATO, AND OTHER ALLIES NEED DUAL-PURPOSE FORCES to cope with limited aggression, even limited nuclear aggression.

D. U.S. MUST ALSO MAINTAIN AN EFFECTIVE STRATEGIC FORCE:

   1. There is no alternative to achieving a retaliatory threat sufficient to deter all-out attack on the U.S. or NATO.
   2. Advanced U.S. weapons technology is necessary to maintain a nuclear stand-off on strategic level.
   3. Should war break out, the U.S. needs the ability to destroy enemy weapons.

IV. RECOMMENDATIONS FOR U.S. MILITARY POLICY.

A. ADHERE TO THE MILITARY IMPLICATIONS OF OUR ESTABLISHED U.S. NATIONAL PURPOSES.

   1. Protect the free world against an all-out attack by the maintenance of secure retaliatory power.
   2. Increase U.S. and allied capability to cope with limited aggression.

B. DETER STRATEGIC NUCLEAR ATTACK.

   1. Assign top priority to reducing vulnerability of American and allied strategic forces.

      a. Increase mobility, concealment, and dispersal of bases to protect bombers, communications and warning systems, control centers, missile launching sites and personnel.

     b. Improve weapons and tactics, etc., to enable even a reduced retaliatory force to reach its targets.

     c. Increase number of SAC planes on "alert" status.

     d. Take civil defense measures that allow as much protection and recovery as possible.

  2. Provide for adequate missile deterrent capacity in mid-60's.

     a. Accelerate development of solid fuel ICBM's, capable of large-quantity production and mobile siting.

     b. Protect missile systems by hardening land missile sites, increasing the use of mobile land, sea and air-based missiles.

C. PREPARE FOR WIDE RANGE OF NONNUCLEAR FORMS OF ATTACK.

  1. Step up American and allied efforts to prepare for lesser forms of aggression, ranging from subversion to conventional attacks, on overseas countries.

  2. Discourage development of nuclear forces by allied nations.

     a. Such independent forces add little to U.S. strategic deterrent and detract from local defense.

     b. *If impossible* to dissuade allies from nuclear development, try to channel allied efforts into mobile or otherwise protected retaliatory systems. (U.S. should share technical information on hardened missile sites and solid missile propellants.)

  3. Maintain adequate levels of dual-purpose forces.

     a. Develop U.S. and European nonnuclear capabilities.

     b. Simultaneously equip American and allied troops with tactical nuclear weapons.

D. MAINTAIN U.S. EFFORTS IN SPACE TECHNOLOGY.

  1. Prevent U.S.S.R. from surpassing the U.S. in new weapons.

  2. Develop a wide range of space vehicles for:

     a. Military purposes, such as intelligence, missile detection.

     b. Nonmilitary purposes such as worldwide communications, television, weather prediction.

E. ATTEMPT TO INCREASE NUCLEAR STABILITY.

  1. Take unilateral action designed to deter opponent's attack.

     a. Reduce vulnerability of our own strategic forces.

     b. Avoid deployment of vulnerable strategic missile systems close to Communist borders.

     c. Reduce reliance on "hair trigger" response mechanisms (e.g., detection systems) conducive to accidental war.

     d. Assume military strategy and policy positions which reduce rather than augment instabilities (e.g., rattling of strategic weaponry).

2. Promote an international arms control arrangement which would supplement nuclear stability by helping control spread of nuclear weapons. Such an agreement should:

   a. Be directed at increased strategic stability, not at total disarmament (which gives decisive advantage to side which develops weapons surreptitiously).

   b. Limit strategic forces to retaliatory systems insufficient for first-strike.

   c. Provide for inspection system. (Further technical work necessary on this prior to agreement.)

   d. Take into account need to negotiate with Communist China on arms control.

Study No. 9

THE FORMULATION AND ADMINISTRATION OF U.S. FOREIGN POLICY

The Brookings Institution
1775 Massachusetts Avenue, N.W.
Washington, D. C.

Published: January 13, 1960

109

GOAL OF THE REPORT

To suggest organizational and administrative changes in the United States government which will be needed to meet the:
a. Conditions created by a continuing cold war.
b. Consequences of rapid scientific and technological advances, especially in weapons.
c. Implications of the rise of the underdeveloped nations.

MAJOR PREMISES OF THE REPORT

1. The U.S. will be one of the major forces shaping the future world environment.
2. The period ahead demands bold adjustment of American institutions, as well as policies and attitudes. The U.S. may suffer reverses unless it improves:
   a. The speed and flexibility of its processes of foreign policy formulation and execution.
   b. Machinery and powers to identify and analyze long-range policy problems.
   c. Its capacity to implement foreign policy goals through better use of national skills, energies and resources.
   d. Collaboration with other friendly countries, through both bilateral and multilateral channels.
3. Major factors influencing future U.S. foreign policy decisions are:
   a. Worldwide scientific advances in atomic and solar energy, nuclear weapons, industrial technology—and increased mobility of goods, ideas and people.
   b. Accelerated world population growth.
   c. Growing U.S. domestic dependence on foreign raw material resources.
   d. Proliferation of new, independent states resulting from the new era of mounting nationalism.
4. Bipartisanship is possible and desirable regarding the most critical aspects of foreign policy. The theory and practice of bipartisanship need clarification.

I. CONGRESS — INSTITUTIONAL MODIFICATIONS.

A. BACKGROUND OF GROWING CONGRESSIONAL FOREIGN POLICY INVOLVEMENT.

    1. Over one-half of the standing committees of Congress deal regularly with issues of international significance.

    2. Need for means to increase internal coordination, as well as knowledge and speed of action, grows with trend toward greater legislative involvement in foreign affairs.

B. RELATIONSHIP OF CONGRESS TO THE EXECUTIVE BRANCH—PROPOSALS:

    1. Both branches should reduce secrecy consistent with essential requirements of national security.

    2. Congress should encourage Executive Branch to bring public into closer touch with policy through:

        a. High-level briefings for selected groups of opinion leaders.

        b. Making information and other services available to public groups and individuals interested in world affairs.

    3. Both branches should increase consultations with non-governmental specialists and opinion leaders.

    4. Channels of information and consultation between the two branches should be strengthened through:

        a. Increasing informal meetings among committees whose activities relate to foreign policy.

        b. Greater use of Congressional liaison staffs.

    5. More regular contact between top leadership of both branches should be developed.

C. INTERNAL CONGRESSIONAL ORGANIZATION FOR FOREIGN AFFAIRS—PROPOSALS:

    1. The Congressional committee.

        a. Periodic briefings should be available to assist Members and their staffs in relating specific committee assignments to broad foreign policy questions.

        b. There should be modest expansion of committee staffs which are closely involved in foreign affairs.

        c. Congress should consider establishing new joint select committee to study national security in order to bring the chairmen and ranking minority members of the principal committees involved in international problems together with the Party leadership, or

        d. As an alternative to the joint select committee, have periodic reviews of national security policy by each foreign policy committee, inviting participation by leading members of other committees.

    e. Foreign affairs specialist staff of the Legislative Reference Service should be expanded.

2. The appropriations process.

    a. Premise: Certain major foreign policy operations, especially foreign aid, have been seriously impaired by:

       (1) Congressional insistence on year-to-year budgeting.

       (2) Frequent lack of coordination among committees with fiscal powers over foreign policy legislation.

    b. Recommendations:

       (1) Appropriate for multi-year programs, with accompanying annual Congressional review.

       (2) Improve coordination between substantive and appropriation committees in order to:

          (a) Relate individual appropriations to broad policy aims.

          (b) Eliminate overlapping research and review.

       (3) Permit greater flexibility in the administration of foreign affairs programs.

II. EXECUTIVE BRANCH — INSTITUTIONAL MODIFICATIONS

A. PROPOSED: MODIFIED SYSTEMS AND STRUCTURES FOR POLICY MAKING AND POLICY EXECUTION.

1. *National Security Council.*

    a. Advisory bodies and Executive Office staff, however competent, are ineffective without decisive leadership and direction from the President. An interdepartmental advisory body should:

       (1) Identify crucial issues.

       (2) Encourage coordination at lower levels.

       (3) Balance evidence and judgments.

       (4) Review approved policies and implementing action.

    b. Policy papers are currently marked by heavy compromise between military and political thinking; thus often lack a clear, long-range foreign policy framework.

    c. Through meetings having better preparation and fewer participants tied to departmental viewpoints, the NSC should achieve:

       (1) A sharper, more imaginative, longer-range analysis of major issues.

       (2) More effective conciliation between substantive and budgetary considerations.

    d. There is need for more closely meshed political and military programming (military programming frequently undertaken on longer-range basis than the total foreign policy of which it is a part).

2. *Operations Coordinating Board.*

    a. Assign OCB Chairmanship to Department of Foreign Affairs (see II-B below).

      b. OCB should concentrate in greater detail on smaller number of issues than at present.

      c. OCB effectiveness should be monitored by independent examining staffs at departmental and Executive Office levels.

  3. *Executive Office staff.*

      a. Better coordination and clearer policies among assistants and staffs most directly concerned with foreign policy demands that:

        (1) Personnel in Executive Office involved with foreign policy and national security be integrated into an Office of National Security Affairs.

        (2) Its Director have status similar to that of the Director of the Budget.

  4. *Better use of non-government research facilities.*

      a. Consider establishing institution for foreign policy planning similar to Air Force-supported Rand Corporation.

      b. Consider taking initial experimental steps to find optimum relationship between government and non-government groups through series of problem-oriented task forces using various administrative formulae.

B. PROPOSED: A NEW "DEPARTMENT OF FOREIGN AFFAIRS."

  1. To promote unified responsibility for the main stream of foreign policy planning and operational control, it is proposed that a Department of Foreign Affairs be created, subordinate to the President, with responsibility for principal political, economic and cultural aspects of foreign policy.

  2. Create new post of *Secretary of Foreign Affairs.*

      a. Principal role to have ultimate control of policy and operations regarding political, economic, and information aspects of foreign policy.

      b. Secretary to serve also as Vice Chairman of the National Security Council.

      c. Office of the Secretary of Foreign Affairs would include small, high-level planning staff.

        (1) This should become a major factor in promoting a conscious government "planning community."

        (2) Staff to possess wider range of skills than now available to it.

        (3) Staff needs to become a principal link to military planners.

        (4) Operations may be supplemented by adding a planning officer to each regional bureau of the State Department.

  3. Department of Foreign Affairs to contain three component Departments, each with considerable autonomy and each headed by a subordinate Secretary.

      a. *Department of State.*

        (1) Secretary responsible for formulation and execution of

"political" sectors of foreign policy (as distinct from military, economic, cultural).

(2) Geographic bureau can be reorganized into more logical geo-political units, e.g.:

    (a) Add Greece and Turkey to European Affairs.

    (b) Create new Bureau of Asian and Pacific Affairs and Bureau of African and Asia Minor Affairs.

    (c) Bureau of Communist Bloc Affairs not recommended.

(3) Bureau of International Organization Affairs to be directly subordinate to Secretary of State.

  b. *Department of Foreign Economic Operations.*

    (1) Current dispersal of foreign economic activities (trade, aid, surpluses, military and monetary policies) is wasteful, inimical to unified planning and diminishes impact of aid.

    (2) International Cooperation Administration, Development Loan Fund and most functions under PL 480 should be merged (Export-Import Bank should remain separate) in order better to:

       (a) Coordinate U.S. government aid programs.

       (b) Integrate country or regional development programs and plan them on a longer-term basis.

       (c) Relate U.S. government aid programs to those of other countries.

    (3) New Department of Foreign Economic Operations would:

       (a) Provide policy guidance to U.S. representatives at the World Bank, International Finance Corporation, International Monetary Fund, the United Nations and the Organization of American States.

       (b) Integrate military aid decisions with those relating to economic aid under general direction of the Secretary of Foreign Affairs.

  c. *Department of Information and Cultural Affairs.*

    (1) U.S. Information Agency should be merged with cultural affairs program of the Department of State.

    (2) As an arm of U.S. foreign policy, these operations should be conducted under the department responsible for their policies.

C. PROPOSED: REVISED RELATIONS BETWEEN FOREIGN AND MILITARY POLICY-MAKING MACHINERY.

  1. Rational foreign and military policies cannot be planned separately—they need to reinforce each other; however, they have frequently been uncoordinated and conflicting.

  2. There should be closer consultation and coordination between members of foreign policy agency and military personnel through:

    a. Increased attendance at war colleges by foreign policy specialists.

      b. Increased personnel exchanges between military and civilian agencies.

      c. Thorough communication on political and military matters between new Department of Foreign Affairs and the Office of International Security Affairs of the Defense Department.

   3. To improve foreign policy relationships of the Department of Defense:

      a. Secretary of Defense should have "military statesman" role, with continuing Office of International Security Affairs separate from Joint Chiefs and military services.

      b. Military services under Joint Chiefs should be permitted to engage in direct contacts with government foreign policy agencies on matters involving operational military matters.

III. EXECUTIVE BRANCH — MODIFICATIONS IN FOREIGN POLICY PERSONNEL PROGRAMS.

A. RECOMMENDATIONS FOR NEW DEPARTMENT OF FOREIGN AFFAIRS.

   1. Establish unified service of career foreign affairs personnel among the three component Departments. This would:

      a. Improve climate for teamwork.

      b. Help harmonize policies among Departments.

      c. Reduce administrative costs and machinery.

   2. Aid and information agencies should work toward common personnel system independently (for the present).

   3. International Cooperation Administration and U.S. Information Agency should seek legislative authority for establishment of a career service similar to Foreign Service.

      a. The established system should permit appointment of outside specialists for *ad hoc* programs.

B. RECOMMENDATIONS FOR FOREIGN SERVICE PERSONNEL PROGRAM.

   1. Develop policies to increase flexibility in career patterns as means to promote specialist as well as generalist skills among career officers.

   2. Have special examinations to facilitate recruitment of specialists in certain fields.

   3. Establish mechanisms to foster a continuous inventory of future personnel requirements.

   4. Further implement Wriston Committee suggestions on recruitment and training.

      a. Promote stable annual rate of junior officer intake.

b. After preliminary security check, grant temporary assignments in order to reduce waiting between orals and final appointment.

c. Establish a graduate-level merit scholarship training program for Service applicants (a more practical and economical device than a government Foreign Service Academy).

d. Expand training program, with minimum of one year of training for every nine in service; mid-career training for all Officers.

e. Expand language and area training facilities.

f. Personnel Office of Department of State should undertake to:

(1) Review Foreign Service Officer rating system with aim to improving methods of evaluation and promotion.

(2) Establish "assignment panel" to help assure objectivity of assignment.

(3) Apply "selection-out" process judiciously. Consider abandoning promotion as requirement for remaining in Service; this might promote:

(a) More rapid advancement of the most competent Officers.

(b) Greater initiative on the part of Officers without jeopardy to jobs.

C. RECOMMENDATIONS FOR U.S. OVERSEAS REPRESENTATION.

1. Premises:

a. Gap is widening between personnel and financial resources on one hand and volume and complexity of burdens upon field staff on the other.

b. Initiative in the field is hampered by restrictions from Washington.

c. Lack of integration of diverse field activities into coherent programs is largely due to uncoordinated independent agencies.

d. Career officers are more likely than non-career appointees to possess required skills.

2. Recommendations:

a. Ambassadors.

(1) Increase ambassadors' financial allowances to permit appointments on basis of merit alone. Eliminate need for men of independent wealth to assume posts in which government allowances are inadequate.

b. Staff.

(1) Increase staff available for overseas duty.

(2) Increase allowable terms of service beyond two years.

(3) Make available more language and area training courses to more officers.

(4) Reduce staff loads.

(a) Wherever possible, transfer appropriate functions to

private groups, other cooperating governments, multilateral organizations.

(b) Reduce volume of required reporting.

(c) Reduce volume of detailed supervision by Washington.

Study No. 10

THE PRINCIPAL IDEOLOGICAL CONFLICTS, VARIATIONS THEREON, THEIR MANIFESTATIONS, AND THEIR PRESENT AND POTENTIAL IMPACT ON THE FOREIGN POLICY OF THE UNITED STATES

Center for International Affairs
Harvard University
6 Divinity Avenue
Cambridge, Massachusetts

Published: January 17, 1960

GOALS OF THE REPORT

1. *To analyze* the role played by ideology in international affairs.
2. *To discuss* the relationship of ideology to U.S. foreign policy.
3. *To describe* the complex and changing relationships among the three dominant political ideologies today: *constitutional democracy, nationalism* and *communism*.

MAJOR PREMISES OF THE REPORT

1. The present era of rising literacy and social expectations has made the effective execution of government policies increasingly dependent upon mass support.
2. As communications improve and relations among nations become more intimate:
    a. The problems of domestic politics and those of foreign relations become increasingly interrelated.
    b. The formulation of foreign policy is increasingly affected by hopes, beliefs and fears of mass populations.
3. Ideology, although very important, is but one of many factors shaping world events.
4. An ideology operates effectively only when it is embraced by an organized movement or embodied by political institutions.
5. An ideology can be incompatible with the social and political environment in which it operates.
6. The content and emphases of an ideology may be reshaped by time and changing circumstances.

I. THE MAIN CONTENDING IDEOLOGIES OF THIS ERA: CONSTITUTIONAL DEMOCRACY, NATIONALISM, COMMUNISM.

A. CONSTITUTIONAL DEMOCRACY.

1. By its very nature, democracy cannot be a precise creed.
2. Democratic tradition does contain within it a body of civic duties, political premises and principles. Among these are:
    a. Belief that the human being is a creature of unique worth with inherent rights to liberty, dignity and a decent economic and social life.
    b. The right of self-government.
    c. The principle of rule of law for protection of individual rights.
    d. Tolerance and welcoming of diverse views, attitudes and values.

    e. Dedication to evolutionary change by non-violent means, with the assumption that change is natural and continuing.

    f. The right of all human beings to achieve the democratic values described above.

3. Security interests have sometimes led the U.S. to compromise democratic principles, by allying with dictatorial regimes or ignoring demands of colonial peoples; this has tended to erode U.S. prestige as a leading constitutional democracy.

B. NATIONALISM.

1. Definition: "Nationalism is the assertion by a people of its claim to a distinctive national identity, entitling it to live its own life in its own fashion."

2. Nationalism seldom yields positive doctrine beyond the demand for a sovereign state, independent of alien overlords.

    a. It tends to be "anti" in character.

    b. While based on mass support, it is not necessarily democratic and frequently leads to autocratic government.

    c. In foreign affairs, nationalist ideology:

        (1) Prescribes no clear policies.

        (2) Can inhibit useful international contact because of distrust and fear of alien intrusion.

    d. Economically, it tends to be restricted to the quest for economic development.

        (1) It provides no guidelines for economic programs.

        (2) Paradoxically, it may lead to policies against the best interests of a country (e.g., restrictions against foreign investment).

3. Nationalism does, however, have much to contribute to the development of new countries, by:

    a. Providing a sense of social and political solidarity.

    b. Injecting dynamism and political activism into the society.

C. COMMUNISM.

1. Marxist-Leninist ideology as adapted by Communist leaders plays a significant role in shaping the foreign policies of the Communist regimes; these policies are also influenced by:

    a. Historic national drives.

    b. Strategic considerations.

2. Major tenets of Communist ideology which are currently relevant to Soviet and Chinese foreign relations are:

    a. The view of the world which sees the "progressive" (Sino-Soviet) forces in irreconcilable conflict with the "reactionary" (Western) forces.

b. The ultimate victory of Communism.

(1) Confidence in this seems to have grown recently to the point where military conflict between Communism and capitalism may no longer be deemed necessary, because the balance will instead be turned by:

(a) The struggle for economic growth in newer nations.

(b) The industrial growth of the Communist nations.

(2) This view would undoubtedly change if it were calculated that military victory were possible without impossible losses.

c. The Communist party is the chosen instrument for achieving the millennium and, as such, is entitled to a monopoly of state power.

d. Acquiring and consolidating power is a central preoccupation of Communist ideology.

e. Tactical flexibility and variableness of strategy with the particular situation are permissible under the Communist creed.

(1) They are possible because the ultimate goals of Communism are essentially vague and remote.

(2) This may result in enunciation in non-Communist areas of policies which seem to contradict basic tenets of the creed.

II. COMMUNISM AND NATIONALISM WITHIN THE COMMUNIST BLOC.

A. SUPREMACY OF THE U.S.S.R. IN THE COMMUNIST BLOC.

1. The majority of regimes within the bloc would be unable to continue in power without Soviet military protection.

a. Thus, only strong indigenous Communist regimes (China, Yugoslavia) can afford to deviate from the Soviet pattern of socioeconomic development.

b. Significant deviation elsewhere is almost impossible to sustain.

2. Communist ideology serves to bind the bloc; the U.S.S.R. claims the role of central interpreter of the ideology in order to:

a. Prevent internal bloc crises over conflicting interpretations.

b. Give proof of bloc unity in the face of a common "capitalist" enemy.

3. The fact of Soviet supremacy engenders hostility to Soviet-supported Communist regimes and provides an element of disunity within the bloc.

B. POLAND.

1. Poland remains a persistent challenge to bloc unity.

a. Premier Gomulka insists Poland must enjoy relative domestic autonomy.

b. Gomulka has repeatedly emphasized that different historical backgrounds in Poland and Russia demand different policies, e.g., in agriculture.

2. Gomulka is, nonetheless, a convinced Communist who believes:
   a. It is possible and desirable for Communist doctrine to be adjusted to particular national circumstances.
   b. Cohesion within the bloc is necessary, even if it entails some sacrifice, as a means of maintaining external unity against dangers of imperialism and capitalism.
   c. Poland is substantially dependent on the U.S.S.R. militarily and politically, particularly for support on Poland's Oder-Neisse border.

C. YUGOSLAVIA.

1. In 1958, Yugoslavia posed a clearcut ideological challenge to the U.S.S.R. and other Communist parties.
   a. It decided, for example, that:
      (1) The world is not divided into two irreconcilable blocs; rather it is an interrelated organic whole in which both capitalist and Communist areas are undergoing an evolutionary change that might eventually bring the two together.
      (2) Communism can be built without the dictatorship of the Communist party.
   b. Yugoslavia's ideological break is regarded by most Eastern European regimes as an irritant more than a threat. It represents for them an extreme alternative, which none of them is presently powerful enough to emulate.

2. Despite its challenge, Yugoslavia remains basically sympathetic to the Communist bloc, believing that eventually socialist and Communist forms of economic organization will prevail over capitalist.

D. THE SATELLITES.

1. Persistent nationalism of the captive peoples of Eastern Europe forces the unpopular Communist elites there to seek continued Soviet support.

2. The political dependence of satellite regimes upon the U.S.S.R. limits their autonomy as well as their capacity for ideological innovation or deviation.

3. Insofar as political change within the satellites is possible or expressible, the direction is toward democratic socialism.
   a. It is now generally realized that revolutionary moves will invoke direct Soviet intervention. (The possibility of Soviet intervention in revolutionary situations would not be precluded by withdrawal of Soviet military forces.)
   b. The satellites would more likely rely on social pressure to achieve change since the experience of the Hungarian Revolution seems to argue against direct Western intervention.

E. COMMUNIST CHINA.

1. While a large degree of ideological unity prevails between the U.S.S.R. and Communist China, there are significant ideological differences.

   a. These differences center on:

      (1) The Maoist conception of revolution, which rests on a standing army and land-hungry peasantry rather than the urban proletariat.

      (2) Mao's reliance on coalition government rather than the dictatorship of the proletariat (i.e., the party).

      (3) Chinese reliance since 1958 on the communes to bring it to the threshold of pure Communism (a stage of transition no other Communist power has claimed to have reached as yet).

   b. The Chinese departure from the U.S.S.R. in ideology and economic organization imposes strains on bloc unity, particularly because of its potential appeal to some satellites.

   c. Where disputes have arisen, compromise between the Chinese and Soviet positions has thus far been achieved.

      (1) The Chinese have in the past taken the lead in insisting on universal recognition of Soviet leadership in the Communist camp.

      (2) The U.S.S.R. has acknowledged China's right to individuality in its domestic politics.

2. Cohesive elements within the Sino-Soviet alliance.

   a. Common aspirations.

   b. Mutual hostility to external world.

   c. Chinese dependence on U.S.S.R. for means of rapid industrialization.

3. Divisive factors and potential elements for disintegration of the alliance.

   a. Progressive weakening of the ideological bond through conflicting interpretations.

   b. Increasing divergence of national interests surmounting ideological ties.

F. MAIN SOURCES OF IDEOLOGICAL EROSION WITHIN COMMUNIST BLOC.

1. It appears to be distinctly possible that, in the long-haul, Communist ideology will be transformed from a revolutionary creed involving self-sacrifice into a doctrine of permanent rule. This trend could create discontent, destroy Communist fervor and impair bloc unity.

2. The industrialization and urbanization of the Communist states need *not* lead to the introduction of democratic government. It may merely give rise to a more rational totalitarian society in

which the use of terror is minimized and which is an even more effective tool for promotion of the international goals of the ruling Communist elite.

III. NATIONALISM IN THE UNDERDEVELOPED AREAS.

A. THE COMMUNISTS TYPICALLY EXPLOIT NATIONALISM for their own purposes.

1. In underdeveloped areas, the Communists cultivate not just the proletariat but also the local intellectuals and even the local capitalists.
2. Before independence is attained, the nationalists borrow from Lenin's *Imperialism* to explain past subjugation. Communists then express willingness to ally themselves with the "anti-imperialist" nationalists.
3. Following the achievement of national statehood:
   a. The nationalists are gradually forced to define their attitude toward Communism.
   b. Communism offers tempting solutions to the problems bedeviling the nationalists.
      (1) Citing Soviet and Chinese success in achieving rapid industrialization, it offers a concrete program for the social and economic development so important to contemporary nationalists.
      (2) It offers a means of coping with the extensive economic and social dislocations resulting from rapid industrialization; this period of upheaval may create a revolutionary situation favorable to a Communist seizure of power.
4. The Chinese Communists are now pushing for a more aggressive policy in underdeveloped areas than the present strategy of waiting for favorable situations for power seizures to develop.

B. NATIONALISM ASSUMES DIFFERENT FORMS in different areas.

1. *India.* The main ideological elements in Indian nationalism are:
   a. Gandhism, which, based on a reformed version of the traditional culture, stresses duty, self-sacrifice, non-violence, anti-materialism, the reshaping of society through the reform of individuals and the obligation of individuals to social groups.
   b. Fabian socialism, which is fundamentally critical of 19th century individualistic capitalism (an economic system Indians tend to believe still exists in the U.S.). This is identified with Nehru.
   c. Constitutional democracy.
   d. Marxism-Leninism, preached by the Communist Party, which has made strenuous efforts in recent years to persuade Indians their Marxism-Leninism is subordinate to and compatible with Indian patriotism.

e. Anti-colonialism and anti-imperialism—the main ideological strands that weave together all others and make Indian nationalists sympathetic to Marxism-Leninism and the U.S.S.R. Chinese aggressions may, however, change these sympathies.

2. *Non-Communist Asia.* Nationalism is still the fundamental principle of political action to which all other ideologies must be subordinated. These nations will form alliances with either big power that will aid them in their feuds with their neighbors.

3. *Arab countries.*
   a. The two elements in nationalism here are:
      (1) Generalized Arab nationalism, based on devotion to Islam.
      (2) Nationalism of the various Arab states created haphazardly after World War I and including heterogeneous ethnic groups.
   b. The Communists have used three non-ideological tactics to promote their cause:
      (1) Associating themselves with the nationalists' "anti" feelings—against "imperialists" and against avaricious and corrupt internal groups.
      (2) Pointing to the U.S.S.R.'s spectacular successes as a model for the achievement of Arab economic goals, and offering Soviet aid.
      (3) Infiltering the Arab governments at all levels.
   c. Three ideological factors the U.S. must consider in making policy toward the Arabs:
      (1) U.S. concept of democracy is not understood by, presently sought by, or presently practical for the Arabs. To avoid conflict the U.S. must recognize Arabs' current need for centralized authority.
      (2) U.S. must exploit U.S.-Arab agreement on the right of national self-determination, an issue which the Communists, of course, avoid.

4. *Latin America.*
   a. In this area of emerging national awareness:
      (1) The peasants and the urban proletariat are becoming politically conscious, and
      (2) Organized labor, the middle classes, and the students are growing rebellious against the upper class which has long dominated political and economic life in most of Latin America.
   b. All of the principal ideological movements are attuned to rising Latin American nationalism and advocate state intervention in social and economic matters:
      (1) *Communism,* because of its anti-Americanism, has a small but influential band of followers (even though the Communist Party is outlawed in many Latin American countries).
      (2) *Fascism* has foundered in Latin America in the 1950's.

(3) *Catholic Action groups* have comparatively slight influence because the Catholic hierarchy is associated in the public mind with the traditional era.

(4) *Democratic socialism and welfare liberalism* have the greatest ideological appeal to Latin Americans outside the upper class.

c. We shall probably see adopted in some Latin American states the Mexican pattern of a one-party government following a kind of democratic socialism. Others, however, are moving toward Chile's multi-party system of democratic government.

C. ALL THESE AREAS have some views in common.

1. Overwhelming desire for rapid economic development has led to an ideological acceptance of some measure of socialism.

2. They tend to view the present world conflict as between two sharply differentiated socio-economic systems:
   a. The U.S. as defender of the status quo these nations oppose, and
   b. The U.S.S.R. as a revolutionary power.

3. In these areas of extremely sensitive nationalist consciousness, there is mounting strain between Communism and nationalism because of Communism's international aspirations and allegiance to the U.S.S.R.

IV. NEUTRALISM IN THE UNDERDEVELOPED AREAS.

A. THE POST-COLONIAL NATIONALISTIC STATES view neutralism as:

1. The reflection of their desire to concentrate on domestic economic development free of military burden.

2. A political necessity dictated by domestic public opinion. Excessive support of the Western position would be the kiss of death to such advocates and, thus, in the long run would benefit the Communists.

3. An opportunity to maximize their international role and compensate for economic and military weakness. The neutralists have developed the tactics of negotiation as a means of increasing their influence in world politics.

4. An opportunity to perform an international service by promoting peace and mitigating differences between the big powers.

B. LATIN AMERICA, while a natural if occasionally uncomfortable ally of the U.S., is increasingly aware of affinities with Asia, Africa, and the Middle East.

1. It can be expected more frequently to take positions at variance with those of the U.S.

2. This, however, is not "neutralism."

C. NATIONS WHICH HAVE NOT YET ACHIEVED INDE-
PENDENCE regard U.S. policy toward them as one of neutrality.
In view of this and particularly considering Soviet willingness to
support their nationalist movements, the most the U.S. can expect is
their continued rejection of Communism and their maintenance of
neutralist positions.

V. INTERNATIONALISM.

A. INTERNATIONALISM HAS NEVER REALLY BEEN AN
IDEOLOGY IN ITSELF, but it is an element in other ideologies.

1. Internationalism today is a corrective, not a substitute, for
nation-states; it is a remedy against the dangers arising when
states are left to their own devices and a cure for the deficiencies
states experience when isolated.

B. EXTENSION OF INTERNATIONAL PROCEDURES has become
essential to the West since World War II.

1. Nationalist revolution has created national units the viability
of which is questionable and which therefore need international
assistance lest they be exploited by the Soviets.
2. International and regional forces try to provide for procedures
mitigating the dangers of present power conflicts and for services
in various technical areas which would otherwise become stakes
in these conflicts.
3. The increasing interdependence of states necessitates transnational organizations.

C. THREE KINDS OF TRANSNATIONAL FORCES are:

1. *The U.N. system.* Despite limitations, it has been able to:
   a. Maintain a frail but lasting link between East and West and to
   intervene to limit conflicts started by lesser powers.
   b. Facilitate the decolonization process and provide important
   technological assistance to the underdeveloped areas.
   c. Develop techniques of truce-making and truce-keeping.
   d. Further the psychological unification of the world.
2. *Regional organizations.*
   a. They have tended to reinforce the interdependence of their
   members through peaceful adjustment of disputes among them,
   through economic and sometimes political cooperation, and, in
   some cases, through actual integration (pooling of resources
   under joint control).
   b. However, their impact on world affairs has been limited by their
   narrow scope and the freedom of action retained by members.

3. *Unorganized transnational forces* (ideologies and non-governmental interest groups) have an ambiguous impact on world affairs. Too often they appear as a transnational weapon of a certain state or as the non-governmental extension of a government's policy.

D. TO PROMOTE INTERNATIONALISM the West must follow these policy lines:

1. Develop deliberate policies to foster integration, because international procedures can be exploited for the increase of power by one state over another instead of for the service of all mankind.

2. Help new nations achieve their independence without excessive violence and proceed to the "social mobilization" of their inhabitants with minimum delay and crises, because progress toward integration seems least difficult to achieve with "settled" nations.

VI. IMPLICATIONS AND RECOMMENDATIONS FOR U.S. POLICY ON KEY ISSUES.

A. U.S. RESPONSE TO THE SOVIET CAMPAIGN FOR "COEXISTENCE."

1. The Soviet "coexistence" campaign is designed to cause the non-Communist world to avoid practical actions in defense and vis-à-vis the newer nations. The Communists, however, are using this period for a vigorous offensive in the economic, political and propaganda areas.

2. To insure an understanding by the free nations of the real meaning of "coexistence" the U.S. must make clear that:

   a. The basic conflict is between human freedom and welfare, on the one hand, and totalitarianism, on the other. The conflict is not between socialism and exploitative capitalism.

   b. The conflict is between a conception of world order based on pluralism and diversity and one based on dogmatic totalitarianism.

   c. The West's primary interest is *not* in maintaining the status quo and supporting entrenched domestic interests which oppose necessary social change.

3. The advanced nations of the West must cooperate to develop a broad, positive program to meet the Communist threat and must make heavy sacrifices to carry it out.

B. U.S. **POLICY TOWARD UNDERDEVELOPED AREAS.** The U.S. should:

1. Foster the continued independence of the underdeveloped countries without, as a general rule, seeking from these nations a formal commitment to the West. Such a commitment might erode the popular support of a government or divert too much of a nation's limited resources from the economic development which may well be more important in the long range than accretion in their military power.

2. Display tolerance for governments which do not follow the Western democratic model as long as the regimes act constructively to cope with the problems of their societies.

3. Tolerate socio-economic forms that differ profoundly from those of the Western world.

4. Foster an international approach to economic aid.

C. U.S. **POLICY TOWARD THE COMMUNIST BLOC.**

1. Over the long run the Communist bloc may undergo these changes.

   a. The dogmatic revolutionary ideology may fade.

   b. Doctrinally rooted hostility toward the West might decline if it were to become clearer to the Soviets that our system was not giving way to theirs, but that both are subject to continuous change.

   c. The ideological erosion thus outlined may increase internal tension within the bloc.

2. To foster Communist ideological erosion the U.S. should:

   a. Refuse to recognize Soviet domination of the satellites as final and should insist that the Communist world is an area of concern to the outside world.

   b. Attempt to deal with existing Communist regimes as if they were independent, without, of course, endorsing them.

   c. Stimulate real exchange (versus formal exchange) with the Communist world, particularly the Communist-ruled European states.

   d. Foster continued economic growth in the U.S. to belie Communist assertions.

D. TO CARRY OUT THE PROGRAM OUTLINED ABOVE, the West needs strong, creative leadership to undertake long-term commitments to affirmative goals. This would be fostered by a statement of principles which guide U.S. policy in our age, issued at a timely moment by the highest authority.

Study No. 11

U.S. FOREIGN POLICY IN THE U.S.S.R. AND EASTERN EUROPE

Harvard-Columbia Research Group
The Russian Institute
Columbia University
New York, New York

Published: February 14, 1960

133

GOALS OF THE REPORT

To analyze major aspects of the military, political, economic and ideological challenge presented by the Soviet Union.

To suggest U.S. postures with regard to Soviet aims to expand control to other nations.

To draw implications from this analysis for future U.S. foreign policy toward the Communist bloc countries.

MAJOR PREMISES OF THE REPORT

1. The primary aim of U.S. foreign policy should be to further the peaceful and productive growth of the non-Communist world.
2. Soviet long-term goals are unlikely to change; Soviet theory and its internal and foreign policies are subject to change, have changed, and may be influenced further to change.
3. The guiding objectives for U.S. counter-strategy must be the promotion of:
   a. Political and economic development within the non-Communist world.
   b. The development of internal machinery for more concentrated and rational use of domestic resources, both military and economic.
   c. Greater flexibility in international relations.
   d. Increased public awareness of the nature, long-term aspects and demands of the struggle.
4. The overriding aim of U.S. policy toward the U.S.S.R. should not be absolute pursuit of peace—since this might lead to surrender to Soviet objectives—but preservation of freedom.

I. ANALYSIS OF THE SOVIET CHALLENGE.

A. SOVIET OPERATING ASSUMPTIONS—LONG-TERM.

1. Every non-Communist country is in one or another stage of an inevitable transition from some form of capitalism to Soviet socialism and communism.
2. This transition process requires active Soviet assistance. The means to be used by the Soviet Union to promote creation of communist states include:
   a. Strategic employment of military, political and economic instruments of warfare.
   b. Alternating policies of "peaceful coexistence" and "cold war" depending on which is most effective at given times.
3. In the conduct of Soviet international relations, "peace" becomes a symbol to connote non-resistance to Soviet aims.

4. Soviet "status quo" connotes:
   a. Western recognition of Soviet right to control territories won during or since World War II.
   b. Western agreement not to interfere with revolutionary change occurring outside the Soviet bloc.
   c. Joint U.S.-Soviet agreement prohibiting change of frontiers by military force.
      (1) This specifically excludes "internal" problems.
      (2) "Internal" problems include Chinese claims on Formosa, Communist moves on border territories such as North Vietnam.

B. SOVIET OPERATING ASSUMPTIONS—THE 1960'S.

1. Within the Soviet bloc.
   a. Soviet leaders assume that bloc industrial and consumer goods production will surpass that of the U.S. within 15 to 20 years. This will lead to:
      (1) Increased competition with Western nations for world markets, particularly in Western Europe.
      (2) An increase in politically oriented trade and aid transactions.
   b. The desired political changes abroad can and should be obtained without resort to war because:
      (1) Soviet military power is being increased, and a balance favorable to the Soviets already exists.
      (2) Absence of war best serves Soviet internal goals for economic development and consolidation of satellite countries.
2. Among advanced industrial nations.
   a. Soviet leaders believe that capitalist economies will be unable to match Soviet growth and will move toward mutual destruction through fierce trade competition.
   b. Soviet policy is aimed at accelerating this decline while encouraging more favorable Western policies toward the Soviet Union.
   c. Soviet trade offers and subtle encouragement of European pacifism and nationalism can seriously weaken Western military and trade alliances.
3. Among underdeveloped areas.
   a. Soviet experience of rapid industrialization has great impact on underdeveloped areas and enhances Soviet world position.
   b. Continued encouragement of nationalist movements through economic and military aid will lead to eventual addition of underdeveloped areas to Soviet bloc.
   c. Short-term Soviet aim is to cause these countries to deny their materials, markets and bases to the West.

C. SOVIET INTERNAL POLICIES.

1. Possible modifications in Communist ideology.
   a. There is no essential contradiction between Communist ideology and economic efficiency.

b. The success or failure of Soviet policy internationally will have a greater influence on Soviet ideology than will domestic developments.

2. Domestic changes introduced since Stalin's death.

    a. Numerous changes have improved living conditions and increased individual freedoms. Most noticeable for average citizens have been:

      (1) Decentralization of administration.

      (2) Subordination of police power.

    b. These changes do not necessarily represent a democratization but may instead be part of an effort to increase efficiency and output by offering incentives for voluntary initiative.

    c. Probable intent of these domestic changes is to:

      (1) Increase allegiance of the population.

      (2) Strengthen party control.

      (3) Further develop Soviet military and economic capabilities.

      (4) Sustain the Soviet commitment to world communism.

D. PROSPECTS FOR SOVIET ORBIT POLICY.

1. Communist China.

    a. This report generally concurs with the observations of the Conlon report (See Study #5) with regard to Soviet relations with Communist China:

      (1) That the Soviet Union and Communist China find the advantages of the alliance outweigh the disadvantages.

      (2) That tensions are likely to increase as China emerges more clearly as an alternate center of power within the bloc.

2. Eastern Europe—satellite countries and East Germany.

    a. Relations with the Soviet Union reflect a clear Soviet primacy.

    b. Change would be possible only under strong local parties not immediately dependent on the Soviet Union for survival.

    c. There will probably develop increased diversity of policy within the bloc as a whole, though not exceeding the limits of Communist tolerance.

    d. The only constructive and lasting changes in Eastern Europe will be those which also develop in the Soviet Union.

II. RECOMMENDED U.S. POLICIES TOWARD THE SOVIET BLOC.

A. U.S. POLICY OBJECTIVES TOWARD THE SOVIET UNION.

1. Minimum U.S. objective—to check expansion of Soviet power and influence—requires a coordinated military, economic, political and cultural effort designed to maintain a strong U.S. position.

2. Maximum U.S. objective—to direct U.S. resources toward the healthy political and economic development of the non-Communist world. This course of action is also likely to promote long-term changes in Soviet expansionist policy.

B. GUIDELINES FOR IMPLEMENTING U.S. OBJECTIVES.

1. U.S. Government should:
   a. Limit concern with Soviet behavior to international situations and not attempt to influence internal organization of the Soviet Union.
   b. Recognize that direct transactions with the Soviet Union are not likely to eliminate the fundamental conflict between the U.S. and Soviet systems.
   c. Constantly weigh the effects of U.S. bilateral dealings with the Soviet Union on the attitudes and policies of our allies.
   d. Be prepared to seek through negotiation the settlement of problems between the Soviet Union and the non-Communist world.
   e. Be prepared to take advantage of contradictions and errors in Soviet actions and policies.
   f. In order to achieve greater degree of rationality, purpose and drive in exploitation of our resources, make fuller use of available administrative agencies, regulatory commissions, government licensing and taxation powers.
   g. Give greater attention to expansion of particular sectors of the U.S. economy than to overall growth. This demands increased budget allocations for:
      (1) Nuclear and conventional weapons.
      (2) Scientific and military research.
      (3) Space and missile programs.
      (4) Foreign aid.
      (5) Domestic programs such as schools and roads.

2. U.S. citizens should:
   a. Develop a steady, unemotional understanding of the fundamental nature of the U.S. conflict with the Soviet Union.
   b. Be prepared to accept alternating periods of tension and relaxation as inevitable expressions of this conflict.
   c. Develop enough maturity and responsibility not to demand quick success but to support a sustained and at times self-sacrificing program of economic growth and resistance to Soviet expansionism.

C. GUIDELINES FOR U.S. MILITARY POLICY.

1. Although prevention of war is a major aim, the absolute pursuit of peace might result in surrender to Soviet objectives. We must therefore consider the preservation of freedoms as the primary U.S. aim.

2. Since the military power relationship between the U.S. and the Soviet Union will have a vital effect on future events, U.S. military activities must seek to:
   a. Confine the conflict with the Soviet Union to areas other than military.
   b. Prepare for minimum losses and ultimate victory if war should come.
   c. Effectively backstop U.S. political and diplomatic positions.

3. Emphasis should be on achieving a deterrent strategic force, capable of retaliation and not dependent for success on first-strike capability.

4. U.S. must strengthen limited war capabilities by:
   a. Stocking more nonnuclear weapons;
   b. Taking civil defense measures to reduce loss of life when cities are not primary targets;
   c. Continuing missile and satellite development, support of NATO and foreign military assistance.

5. U.S. should act to break the disarmament and arms control deadlock by:
   a. Applying further resources to research on their technical aspects.
   b. Viewing present nuclear test ban talks not as step toward disarmament but as cooperative effort with the Soviet Union to forestall, postpone or make more costly the acquisition of nuclear weapons by other countries.

D. GUIDELINES ON SPECIFIED AREAS OF EAST-WEST CONFLICT.

1. Berlin.
   a. U.S. must continue to guarantee the independence of West Berlin. Without this guarantee, the will of West Germany to resist Soviet pressure will be seriously weakened.
   b. Though it must recognize the difficulty of unification of Germany, U.S. must not give formal sanction to its division.
   c. Disengagement will not improve chances for German unification.
   d. To ensure peace in Europe U.S. should concentrate energies on the economic and political vitality of Western Europe and all NATO countries.

2. Eastern Europe.
   a. U.S. should continue to consider Eastern Europe as a legitimate area of concern, but should not actually encourage internal crises.
   b. U.S. should encourage autonomy of decision for this as well as all other areas, and refuse to acknowledge the permanence of the Soviet imposed status quo in Eastern Europe.
   c. U.S. should encourage gradual loosening of repressive Soviet control by accurate reporting of conditions in this area and by supporting contacts and exchanges with Eastern Europeans.

3. Middle East.
   a. U.S. must expect continued Soviet competition for political and economic influence in this area.
   b. In view of mutual interest of U.S. and Soviet Union in reducing danger of a war starting in this area:
      (1) The two powers might set limits on U.S.-Soviet military competition there.
      (2) This might involve an enforceable provision barring shipment of arms to the Middle East.
4. Asia and Far East.
   a. It is possible that the Soviet Union is also anxious to insure against war in this area.
   b. Private exploratory diplomatic discussion between the Soviet Union and U.S. on ways to contain such issues as Formosa, Vietnam, Chinese-Indian border dispute might well be fruitful.
5. Trade.
   a. U.S. could use offers to expand trade with the Soviet Union as a lever in its overall bargaining position, since U.S. is not dependent on such trade.
   b. In trade with the Soviet Union U.S. must protect economic interests of its allies.
   c. U.S. should not assume that expanded trade will greatly lessen its fundamental conflict with the Soviet Union.
6. Nonaggression pacts, such as one suggested between NATO and Warsaw Pact countries would not provide real assurance against the use of force without adequate provision for inspection and enforcement.
7. Cultural exchange should be encouraged since it offers U.S. a long-term channel of contact which could have a cumulative, healthy effect on Soviet bloc.
8. Nonpolitical cooperation, as joint medical and scientific research should be encouraged, even though its probable effects on basic Soviet-U.S. differences are limited.

Study No. 12

ECONOMIC, SOCIAL, AND POLITICAL CHANGE IN THE UNDERDEVELOPED COUNTRIES AND ITS IMPLICATIONS FOR UNITED STATES POLICY

Center for International Studies
Massachusetts Institute of
    Technology
50 Memorial Drive
Cambridge, Massachusetts

Published: March 30, 1960

GOALS OF THE REPORT

1. *To outline* the transition toward modernization taking place in the under-developed countries.
2. *To define* the American interest in the course and outcome of this modernization.
3. *To offer recommendations* for U.S. policy toward these countries.

MAJOR PREMISES OF THE REPORT

1. The transition into new economic, political and social forms taking place in underdeveloped countries will inevitably assume varying patterns and take varying lengths of time.
2. There are four interrelated areas of administration and attitude in underdeveloped, "transitional" societies which require change as a prerequisite to development into modern, peaceful, non-totalitarian societies—psychological, political, social and economic.
3. In each case the transition from a traditional to a modern society can be significantly affected by what the U.S. does or does not do.
4. This growth of new nations will significantly alter the economic, political and social environment in which American society must operate.
5. It is distinctly in the U.S. interest to encourage and aid development of independent, peaceful, responsible and non-totalitarian governments.
6. The principal instruments available to the U.S. for influencing the modernization process are economic.

I. RECOMMENDATIONS FOR FUTURE U.S. POLICY FOR THREE CATEGORIES OF UNDERDEVELOPED AREAS.

  A. CATEGORY A: "Traditional" or "near-traditional" societies*—includes most of Africa south of Sahara, more backward parts of Middle East and certain Latin American countries.

   1. In countries comprising this group only small numbers of the elite are aware of requirements for modernization (see premise #2 above).
   2. Basic needs of "Category A" societies are for:
      a. Literacy and popular participation in national life.
      b. Modern economic and political institutions with entrepreneurs and civil servants to man them.
      c. Agricultural planning to increase productivity.

---

* The report ascribes the following main characteristics to "traditional" societies: primacy of agriculture, social prestige and political influence based on land control, limited technology, and lack of adaptability to new circumstances.

      d. Modern systems of transport, power, public utilities.

      e. Accelerated application of modern technology to goal of developing select natural resources in order to increase exports and earn foreign exchange necessary for modernization.

  3. Main tasks of U.S. policy should be:

      a. To communicate U.S. desire to promote modernization.

      b. To survey priority tasks and resources available for performing them.

      c. To provide for build-up of human resources by offering educational and administrative training to individuals from all groups of the society.

      d. To assist in building schools, technical, financial and agricultural institutions.

      e. To provide capital for such basic projects as transport, power, etc.

B. **CATEGORY B**: Typified by Egypt, Iran, Pakistan, Indonesia.

  1. This group is characterized by centralized governments, commitment by leaders to modernization and lack of effective programs for economic, political and social development.

  2. Basic needs of Category B societies are those of Category A nations, plus detailed projection of nations' goals in order to:

      a. Focus energy and leadership talent on sustained modernization efforts, and

      b. Provide constructive opportunities for newly trained citizens to participate in development programs.

  3. Main tasks of U.S. policy should be:

      a. To help leadership groups reach a consensus of nation's aims.

      b. To induce central governments increasingly to move into roles now played by foreign experts who advise and guide state and provincial governments.

      c. To make more U.S. aid available on long-term basis and encourage land reform as part of an overall development effort.

      d. To encourage local military establishments to undertake constructive development tasks such as road building.

C. **CATEGORY C**: Typified by India, Turkey, Argentina.

  1. These societies are already committed to take-off into sustained growth and have detailed development program with sufficient human and social overhead resources to carry them out, provided substantial foreign capital is made available.

  2. Basic needs of these societies are those of Category A and B nations, plus need for:

      a. Mobilization of enough foreign capital and technical assistance to permit simultaneous advance in multiple areas of the economy.

144

      b. Assurance of foreign assistance if catastrophe strikes such crucial areas as food production, etc.

      c. Maintenance of a unified national development plan together with decentralized economic development to encourage growth of private enterprise.

    3. Main tasks of U.S. policy and of entire free world should be:

      a. To insure sufficient supply of foreign exchange during the take-off period.

      b. To make clear the American determination to oppose any attempt at aggression by these nations.

D. SPECIFIC RECOMMENDATIONS FOR U.S. POLICY TOWARD INDIA (which contains 40% of the population of all underdeveloped areas):

    1. Organize free world aid to India to provide over $1 billion per year from all sources during period of third five-year plan.

    2. Guarantee large scale U.S. food and fiber surplus grants to allow increased employment in public projects and to relieve possibilities of inflation due to local crop failures.

    3. Promote spread of high-productivity agricultural techniques among peasantry.

    4. Support the public sector of the economy to insure adequate production of materials and supply the demand necessary to encourage growth of private enterprise.

    5. Search for ways to meet relatively small foreign exchange needs of private business ventures which are essential for continuing growth after the take-off.

II. RECOMMENDATIONS FOR U.S. ECONOMIC, DIPLOMATIC, INFORMATION AND MILITARY POLICY.

A. OVERALL POLICY. U.S. should:

    1. Adapt its basic programs and policies for underdeveloped areas to unique problems of each nation.

    2. Improve coordination in Washington and abroad of diplomatic, economic, military and informational policies toward each country.

    3. Take into account indirect as well as immediate consequences of action in any one field (economic, political, social effects of military assistance).

    4. Recognize long-term nature of modernization process by guaranteeing economic assistance for considerably longer period than at present.

B. ECONOMIC POLICY.

1. *Technical assistance:* Selection of project and personnel is more important than number of dollars allocated.

   a. Goal of U.S. technical assistance should not be confined to imparting specialized knowledge. Technical assistance personnel should also strive to create a core of dedicated indigenous professionals to promote permanent, financially independent public institutions able to cooperate with U.S.

   b. Present tours of duty should be lengthened to insure better adaptation of modern techniques to particular country needs.

   c. All programs should aim toward transmitting skills to local population, which calls for an analysis of education requirements.

   d. Great care should be taken to sponsor agriculture and small-scale business programs so as to include the population outside of the urban areas in the modernization process.

2. *Amount and means of U.S. aid:* Main goal of aid is to encourage underdeveloped countries to promote their own development.

   a. Unless U.S. financial aid is made contingent upon evidence of long-range carefully planned economic programs, underdeveloped countries will tend to request aid to meet crisis situations and ignore necessity for long-term internal development programs.

   b. U.S. must invest in aid from $1.5 to $2 billion more per year than at present in order to effect any rise in the growth rate of per capita income in underdeveloped countries.

      (1) This amount can be effectively utilized immediately, particularly in Category C countries.

      (2) Some local currency repayment must be accepted.

   c. Larger, long-term Development Loan Fund project grants must be offered, particularly to Category A and B countries in return for their promise to devote 5 to 10 years to such investments as public utilities, irrigation, etc.

   d. U.S. assurance of available surplus food and fiber shipments will encourage these countries to shift manpower from agriculture to work on project development.

   e. Vital small business activity should be encouraged by making a sufficient supply of foreign currency available to development institutions within the recipient country to finance relatively low needs of small-scale private investors.

   f. To promote international trade, U.S. should endorse liberal trade policies and discontinue the Development Loan Fund lending policy which requires the borrower to purchase U.S. goods.

3. *Assistance to land reform:* American influence can be only marginal in this critical area but U.S. should not neglect any opportunity to promote reform.
   a. U.S. should strongly back land reform efforts with technical and capital assistance where a government takes the lead in land reform.
   b. U.S. should use its influence to interest large landowners in modernization process and consider giving financial assistance to governments wishing to buy out large landowning interests for purposes of land reform.
4. *International organization of aid:* It is essential to coordinate potential sources of assistance, but it is neither feasible nor desirable to channel sources of capital into an international agency because:
   a. It is doubtful whether parliamentary bodies of lending nations would make sufficient aid available to attack the problem.
   b. Donor countries may not have parallel objectives in giving aid.
   c. New international institutions tend to be created without the old being abolished.
5. *Coordination of aid:* It is more appropriate to establish machinery for coordinating economic assistance among agencies now in operation.
   a. Coordinate national programs by joint meetings between representatives of donor nations and recipient countries.
   b. Coordinate area programs according to regional investment and trade groupings such as that of Colombo Plan countries.
   c. Coordinate donor countries through possible revision of OEEC, with addition of U.S., Canada and perhaps Japan to plan combined underdeveloped area investment. Soviet bloc could be invited to join only after a successful organization has been established.
   d. Lender countries should also plan a forum for the exchange of views between all donor and all recipient nations.

C. DIPLOMATIC POLICY. Ambassador should:
   1. Be given responsibility for the entire range of American activities in the field.
   2. Also have wide discretion to interpret policy directives.
   3. Be aware of heritage and customs of country to which he is assigned and be prepared to offer U.S. help in developing country's own version of responsible government.

D. INFORMATION POLICY.
   1. Major objective should not be the spread of propaganda about life in the U.S., but information about technical, political, and other aspects of modernization process.

2. U.S. should promote local communication, educational facilities and exchange of persons.

E. MILITARY POLICY. (Report deals with the military only to suggest some ways in which military measures may contribute to constructive modernization.) U.S. military assistance should:

1. Contribute to preserving independence and political stability and should not be given to repressive regimes, thus causing American government to be labelled as supporter of a regime which will ultimately be overthrown.

2. Employ financial and human resources in economic and social development abroad and at the same time encourage underdeveloped nations to utilize their military resources to assist in such major development tasks as road construction, irrigation, surveying.

3. Help design and assist training of local armed forces.

4. Provide wider opportunities for foreign military officers to travel and study in the U.S. and broaden our officer programs for foreigners to include civilian-military relations, potential use of army in economic and social development, etc.

5. *Military policy for Africa:*

   a. Unique opportunity for bypassing the large financial burden of a military establishment exists in Africa.

   b. U.S. could take initiative for an international convention— possibly under the U.N.—to guarantee African states against aggression and to prohibit delivery of arms except those needed to maintain internal order. This would free limited funds within these countries for full scale economic development.

Study No. 13

U.S. FOREIGN POLICY IN THE MIDDLE EAST

Staff, Committee on Foreign
    Relations
United States Senate
Senate Office Building
Washington, D. C.

Published: June 9, 1960

GOAL OF THE REPORT

To review the forces, problems and conflicts which over the last 15 years have kept the Middle East in a state of turmoil and which continue to make this region dangerously unstable.

MAJOR PREMISES OF THE REPORT

1. Arab nationalism is a major theme in the Middle East. It gives a degree of unity to events and shapes somewhat the principal forces and conflicts of the area.
2. It is important to Western interests, as well as to the Middle East itself, that Middle Eastern stability be promoted; this can best be done by pressing for a solution to the Arab refugee problem and other fundamental regional conflicts.
3. The Arab refugee problem is not insoluble. Its solution is essential to both normalization of Arab-Israeli relations and Middle East stability generally.
4. Egypt is the key state in the Middle East. Nasser alone has the supreme political power at home and the position in the Arab world to develop substantial Arab unity and Middle East stability.
5. Relative to the Soviet Union, and mainly because of Soviet mistakes, the U.S. has experienced a moderate rise in prestige in the Middle East since the low point of 1956 and 1957.

I. THE MEANING OF THE TERM "ARAB NATIONALISM" AND ITS RELATIONSHIP TO THE GOAL OF MIDDLE EAST UNITY.

A. ARAB NATIONALISM BASED ON ASSERTION OF ARAB DIGNITY.

1. The peoples of the Arab world seek to recover the dignity they feel was lost during centuries of foreign domination.
2. The Arabs are agreed upon this goal, although divided on the means of achieving it.

B. FACTORS PROMOTING ARAB DISUNITY.

1. Arab nationalism is not in itself adequate for the achievement of Arab unity.

2. No two Arab leaders can agree on a form of federation.

    a. President Nasser has been unable to achieve his main goal of converting Arab nationalism into a unity of Arab states, despite his position as the most powerful political leader in the Middle East.

        (1) The Nasser-inspired union of Egypt, Syria and Yemen into a United Arab Republic (U.A.R.) is largely a paper association.

        (2) The U.A.R. is unlikely to become a genuine social-political-economic federation in the near future.

    b. The independent Arab states of Iraq, Jordan and Lebanon have not shown any desire to federate.

        (1) Being non-viable economically and only somewhat more viable politically, Jordan may in fact be required ultimately to merge with a neighboring state.

C. FACTORS PROMOTING ARAB UNITY

1. Nationalism as a unifying force. To a limited degree, Arab nationalism does perform as a unifying force, binding together different Arab countries at different times on such issues as:

    a. Foreign imperialism.

    b. Israel.

    c. Non-alignment policies.

2. Religion as a unifying force.

    a. Islam does provide a unifying force in the Middle East in that:

        (1) It ties the majority of the people to a common tradition.

        (2) It contributes to Arab nationalism.

    b. Islam is not, however, a central political force, primarily because it has not proved pertinent to modern problems.

3. Regional economic development as a unifying force. Such programs could provide the greatest single and most realistic approach to federation in the Middle East.

    a. Regional development programs might begin with Egypt and Iraq and gradually take in all Arab states, possibly even extending to Israel.

    b. President Nasser's great political prestige and his desire for unity of all Arab states could ultimately bring about achievement of such programs—though his chief concern at present seems to be the internal development of the U.A.R.

    c. Egypt and Iraq could benefit one another's economies through cooperative exploitation of resources, if their traditional antagonisms could be overcome.

        (1) The Iraqi population is one-fourth that of Egypt, its agricultural potential is greater than Egypt's.

        (2) Of all Arab states, Egypt possesses a trained corps of civil servants, technicians and engineers. Yet Egypt's economic growth is severely handicapped by the need to maintain large military forces and for other reasons rising out of her political problems.

II. PALESTINE REFUGEE PROBLEM.

A. THE PROBLEM OF THE APPROXIMATELY ONE MILLION ARAB REFUGEES is at the heart of the Arab-Israeli quarrel.

B. ARAB POSITION.

1. Arabs refuse to consider any proposal not allowing for repatriation.
   a. This is regarded as an article of faith, therefore not subject to negotiation.
   b. U.N. General Assembly has supported this principle.
2. Arabs demand adequate compensation for loss of property and years wasted in refugee camps.

C. ISRAELI POSITION.

1. Israel refuses to consider even limited repatriation because of:
   a. Fear that returnees would constitute an Arab fifth column.
   b. Unwillingness to absorb returnees for economic, demographic reasons.
2. Israel has offered compensation to refugees within international agreement.

III. SOVIET MIDDLE EAST POLICY.

A. MAJOR GOALS OF SOVIET FOREIGN POLICY IN THE MIDDLE EAST:

1. To gain political-economic hegemony over as wide an area as possible.
2. To obtain a warm water port on the Persian Gulf.

B. MAJOR IMPEDIMENTS TO PURSUIT OF SOVIET MIDDLE EAST POLICY:

1. Internal Middle East rivalries, particularly between Egypt and Iraq.
   a. Following a high point in Soviet influence after Suez, events have conspired to reduce Soviet prestige.
   b. Soviet relations with the U.A.R. have been weakened because of deep commitments to Iraq.
   c. While the Soviet Union continues aid to Egypt, Nasser has displayed a sincere desire to expand trade with the West.
2. Necessity of reacting swiftly to unpredicted events prevents the Soviets, as it does the U.S., from planning detailed policy. Consequently:
   a. Soviets have proved thus far incapable of formulating a flexible, long-term plan for take-over of the Middle East.
   b. Soviets refrained from making a major play for Iraq, probably for fear of offending nationalist movements in Asia, Africa and Latin America.

IV. U.S. MIDDLE EAST POLICY — RECOMMENDATIONS.

A. U.S. MUST PROMOTE MIDDLE EAST STABILITY.

1. This should be regarded as our paramount goal.
2. U.S. should act in concert with other Western powers to:
   a. Make financial assistance available, with no strings attached, to countries individually or regionally.
   b. Respect strong Middle Eastern non-alignment and anti-imperialist sentiment by:
      (1) Refraining from attempts to impose political influence.
      (2) Continuing to support Asian and African countries which maintain policies of neutrality and aspire to self-determination, taking account of the favorable effect of Western policy toward India.

B. U.S. MUST IMPROVE FACILITIES FOR MIDDLE EAST OBSERVATION.

1. U.S. should greatly increase the number of trained observers in the Middle East to:
   a. Prevent gaps in intelligence information.
   b. Meet the grave challenge posed by the Soviet Union, which trains large numbers of area and language specialists for duty in all Middle East countries.
2. U.S. should provide for rapidly increasing the number of Arabic-speaking foreign service officers.
   a. At present, the corps contains 107 Arab-speaking officers.
   b. State Department estimates a need of 231 such officers.

C. SOLUTION OF THE PALESTINE REFUGEE PROBLEM MUST BE FOUND.

1. Settlement of this problem is essential to improvement of Arab-Israeli relations and to Middle East stability as a whole.
2. Requirements for negotiating settlement of the refugee problem are:
   a. *Israeli diplomatic concession:* acceptance of the principle of repatriation, as set forth by UN resolutions.
   b. *Arab practical concession:* willingness to absorb those refugees (probably more than 90%) not choosing to be repatriated.
   c. Conviction by Nasser or his successor that:
      (1) Settlement will benefit Egypt and other Arab countries.
      (2) Israelis are sincere in willingness to reach settlement.
   d. Egyptian-Iraqi agreement on the issue.
3. Proposed solution of the problem:
   a. U.N. Palestine Conciliation Commission, already instructed to make further study of the refugee solution, should:
      (1) Broaden its membership to include not only U.S., France

and Turkey, but also countries such as Canada, Italy, Sweden; a Latin American country, and possibly Iran.

(2) Bring up to date all relevant information and viewpoints as- a basis for settlement of the problem.

(3) Perhaps appoint a subcommission, having broad geographic spread and special competence in complex and sensitive matters, to help it perform its work.

b. U.N. should establish refugee resettlement machinery:

(1) Using the Palestine Conciliation Commission as a nucleus organization, or

(2) Setting up a separate refugee resettlement commission.

c. There should be provision for repatriation of refugees according to an annual quota limitation.

d. A special fund should be established to help finance resettlement of those refugees not choosing to be repatriated.

e. A long-term, low-interest international loan should be offered to Israel to help finance compensation obligations.